The Netherlands – Circa 1850

TERSCHELLING

GRONINGEN

HATTEM

BERGEN

HAARLEM

AMSTERDAM

VIANEN

THE HAGUE

UTRECHT

LEIDEN

ARNHEM

DELFT

's-HERTOGENBOSCH

25 km

Three Centuries

To Mother Hester and Father Jan

M. C. van Hall

Three

Centuries

The Chronicle of a Dutch Family

Translated from the Dutch
by Michael C. van Hall

Xlibris, Indianapolis, USA 2018

Translation copyright @ 2016 Michael C. van Hall
Originally published in the Netherlands as *Drie Eeuwen* by Uitgeverij W. Ten Have, N.V., Amsterdam 1961.

The Library of Congress has catalogued the original edition as follows:

Library of Congress Cataloging-in-Publication Data Printed in the Netherlands
Hall, Maurits Cornelis van, 1901–1963
Drie Eeuwen
Pages.cm
1. Van Hall Geschiedenis, 2. Bibliographie
LC classification CS829 .H25 1961
61041612

Library of Congress Control Number:	2016912509
ISBN:	Hardcover	978-1-5245-2987-1
	Softcover	978-1-5245-2986-4
	eBook	978-1-5245-2985-7

Print information available on the last page.

Rev. date: 05/29/2018

To order additional copies of this book, contact:
Xlibris
1-888-795-4274
www.Xlibris.com
Orders@Xlibris.com
734788

CONTENTS

The Origin of
the Family

ARNHEM, LEIDEN, AND VIANEN

When Gijsbert van Hall, Esq., some years ago was appointed mayor of Amsterdam, many articles appeared in newspapers about the Van Halls. Gijsbert was called a scion of a distinguished dynasty, and a newspaper amusingly followed this up with an article trying to answer the question: "When does one become a scion? Is a baby already one, or does one become one at a later age? Can one lose his scionship, and if yes, why?"

As members of the family, we carefully read the reports; there was also much news for us.

We noticed that the great-grandfather of the author and the mayor had "A. M. C. van Hall, Esq.," in common, though the whole press, with the exception of the Reformed, kept quiet about that and rather focused on F. A. Baron van Hall, Esq., his oldest half brother. This A. M. C. van Hall, after a turbulent life, died young. He and his wife came in contact with the Justice Department a couple of times—perhaps a reason for his descendants to lose their scionship!

Our curiosity was whetted, and we began to nose around in old archives and writings. In the yellowed journals and letters, vague figures started to appear. One clue led to another, and slowly our forefathers took on firmer forms until they stood in front of us and began to tell us about their lives and their goals—not only the ponderous subjects but also the more intimate and domestic events. They told us much, and in the following pages, the reader will find their story—a story with a laugh and a tear.

ARNHEM

First of all, we started looking for the origin of the family, and we ended up in Arnhem. In the sixteenth century, various Van Halls lived there. They were farmers, gardeners, bakers, and ministers. Where does the name *Van Hall* come from? Most likely, a farm boy settled in the neighborhood, and in answer to the question "Where do you come from?" he answered "From Hall," a hamlet not far from Brummen.

Around 1570, in a homestead in Malburghen below Huissen, a Jan van Hall was born. Malburghen lies on the left side of the Rhine, opposite Arnhem. His son was named Floris Janz (born 1600), and his son's son was Allert Florisz.

This Allert Florisz courted Naletien Teunissen. She lived in a homestead next to the Klingenbeek. The Klingenbeek runs from the hills above Oosterbeek to the Rhine, and in an old print, we could see that there was enough water for the mill next to the homestead. The water mill has since disappeared, and now the crystal clear brook runs through the laundry service of Cramer.

Naletien lived close to the Rhine, and it was not easy for Allert to row his boat from Malburgen to visit her. In 1660, they married and settled along the Klingenbeek. A year later, their son Floris Allertsz was born, and we note him as the first member in the family tree.

Floris Allertsz was just twenty when he decided to immigrate to Leiden, which was a long journey during that time. He hoped to find a better future there than on the Klingenbeek. It shows his entrepreneurship. As the oldest son, yet he forfeited by his departure the chance to inherit the farm and the water mill, which ended up, in 1724, in the hands of his niece Aaltje Weggelaar.

How he traveled from Arnhem to Leiden, he does not mention, but it most likely was by boat and not by carriage. After all, he needed every penny to settle himself in Leiden. Floris Allertz found work in a sheet factory, and after a couple of years, he had accumulated enough capital to go into the landscaping business, the occupation of his ancestors. He became a vegetable grower.

He married Aaltje de Wilde in 1692 and died in 1709.

Floris Allertz left behind an eleven-year-old son, Adriaan, and a little daughter. Financially, he did not do badly; his wife was able to give their children a good upbringing.

In 1720, Adriaan, twenty-two years old, was asked by Jan Aegidius van Egmond van den Nijenburg, Esq., Lord of Egmond and Rijnegom, to accompany him as his secretary on a voyage to the Mediterranean Sea and the Middle East. Lord Van Egmond was the Advisor and Member of the Town Council on Commerce and the Ships of the City of Leiden and was named as "Special Envoy of the Netherlands State" to the Court of Naples. This voyage took four years. The adventures that the gentlemen experienced were candidly and succulently described in a book that appeared a few years later. In it is described the "required" study of the members of the fairer sex of the various countries visited, and we assume that the young Adriaan contributed his proper share to the project. This already started on the island of Terschelling, where adverse winds delayed their departure for several weeks. It was the custom there that young men made out with young daughters by visiting them late at night in their bedrooms. They did not use the front door but climbed into their windows. This happened with the approval of the parents. On one of the nights, it started snowing, and the next morning, Lord Van Egmond and Adriaan van Hall clearly saw all the footprints leading to the various bedrooms, which caused the inevitable amusement of the bystanders.

In the book, serious warnings are given not to have intimate relations with Spanish women. Spanish men are by nature very jealous and won't hesitate to draw a saber or a dagger; they do not have to fear imprisonment as long as it involves the protection of the honor of a female.

Adriaan also diligently assisted his benefactor in his political and commercial mission. After returning to the homeland, Lord Van Egmond gave him as a reward for his services the shipping services between Leiden and Gouda and, later on, also the route to Delft. This was a lucrative and monopolistic enterprise. Almost all the transportation occurred over water. Roads were used rarely, and the railway would not come into existence for a long time. He could let the work be done by someone else and keep the profits for himself. Adriaan profited from this until he died at the age of eighty-five.

His relationship with Van Egmond brought an important change in the position of the family. Before, they were small, self-employed people; now they associated with the regents with all the corresponding advantages. This privilege was something Adriaan got through dedication and intellect and not through marriage, which in those days was the more usual way. His son Floris Adriaan, who we will shortly follow to Vianen, earned his commercial success through his marriage with Anna van Noorle.

In 1726, Adriaan married Sara de Keyzer. We read in various writings that Sara descended from Admiral Piet Hein. This was a little delicate, if this was true, as Piet Hein did not have any legal offspring. Most likely, it was an uncle of the admiral. Adriaan died in 1783.

Some years ago, we visited his last resting place in the Groene of the Willebrordkerk in Oestgeest, one of the oldest churches in our country, next to the freeway Leiden–Amsterdam. The sexton brought us into the church and showed us the mortared gravestone of Adriaan, his wife, and his daughter, which is set in the floor. After we spent a few seconds in reverential silence, the sexton opened an adjacent hatch and proudly showed us the new concrete cellar for the central heating system, which stretches out under all the gravestones. The physical remains of our forefathers were the victims of the ever-forward-rolling technology.

One of his sons, Jan, had a craving for adventure and strange countries, and he effected his impulse in a strange and peculiar way. After he went through four marriages, he left on a sailing vessel with a significant amount of money to retire in the country of Bengal. He died after a "lonely and idle existence." We are not going to disturb his peace but focus on his son Floris Adriaan.

VIANEN

Floris Adriaan van Hall was born in 1736 in Leiden.

To get an impression of the circumstances and atmosphere in which young Floris would find himself, we traveled to Vianen for a further investigation.

This sovereign and free entity (*Vrije Hoogheerlijkheid*) has always occupied a special place in the Low Lands. So it happened that Vianen, during the war of 1672 and to the inconvenience of the States of Holland, signed a neutrality pact with Louis XIV.

For centuries, the Brederodes held sway. They lived in the mighty castle Batestein, which covered a surface area of five acres and against which the heavily fortified little city was built. Emperor Karel V stayed there, and many members of the House of Orange were frequent guests.

The sovereign gentlemen had absolute power. They owned the region along the river Lek and the Zederikkanaal, which covered the north–south traffic. They owned the right to store and then sell certain products for the people (*stapelrecht*). They owned the right of the wind, they owned the mills where wheat had to be milled, and they had the fishing rights and the hunt. Further, they had the exclusive right of burials, the right to strike their own coins—frankly, there are too many to enumerate.

After the Brederodes died out, Carel Count Dohna inherited the estate, and in 1686, it passed to Simon Hendrik Count Lippe, a family member of His Royal Highness Prince Bernhard.

The Lippes stayed in Detmold, Germany, which gave the local magistrates in Vianen enormous power. They, after all, established the local laws and executed them. The various posts were assigned to family members and friends. At times, large sums were paid to get certain posts, and this took on dubious forms; an example of this is when the collection of taxes was farmed out to the highest bidder. The allotter made sure he took care of himself, which occasionally caused uproars.

The Lippes did not receive much pleasure from their new property. There was a burden of debt of half a million guilders, and an interest of twenty thousand guilders was due every year. Dike breaches and floods caused poverty for the peasants, and it was difficult to find the money needed for any restorations.

Among the creditors were various regents—such as Boreel, Schorer, and Trip—and it was understandable that in 1725, Count Lippe, to get rid of the debt, sold Vianen to the States of Holland.

This sale caused the inevitable dismay among the gentlemen of Vianen. During the conveyance, Mayor Dortmont stepped up and asked, "Will the new gentlemen preserve the old laws and privileges?" The representative of the States, Count Hompesch, with his hand on his sword, solemnly declared that this would occur.

The States, in general, kept their promise, although the privilege of safe conduct caused them much annoyance. One could buy in Vianen for one hundred guilders a pardon for a crime and also safe conduct. Thus occurred the odd situation that an offense committed in Holland, even if it was a capital crime, could be bought off with the approval of the States' free gentlemen. Thieves who brought along their assets were doubly welcome. The gentlemen of Vianen were less accommodating on crimes committed in their region. Thereof attested the gallows, which, when the occasion demanded it, was built next to the city hall; the condemned person was led through the open window on the second floor to the gallows and, in view of the assembled people in the wide Voorstraat, hanged.

Only in 1781 did the States abolish this unique privilege. And still during the turbulent years till the absorption by Holland in 1795, it was industriously practiced. One of our forefathers wrote in his daybook about this latter period, and he stated that many examples and names of the participants were known to him. To our regret, he was too discreet to mention them.

The States started to put their house together with a focus on finances. They appointed Herman van Noorle as steward of the Dominion; he was also a bailiff and substitute sheriff.

And so Floris found his bed well made when he, in 1759, at the age of twenty-three, got engaged to Herman's daughter, Anna van Noorle.

To provide him with an income and to facilitate the wedding, he was appointed sheriff of Vianen. With this first position, there followed others: notary, extraordinary vassal (*ordinaris leenman*), bailiff, and count of the dikes (*dijkgraaf*). He lived in Monikkenhof, a remnant of a cloister that was just outside of the gates of the city. He lived a life that was prosperous and quiet—apart from his escape to Amsterdam in 1787, when the Prussians closed in and plundered his house. Although a patriot, he shortly thereafter returned as if nothing had happened and even got some additional positions.

The current mayor of Vianen, Mr. Pellikaan, took us on a guided tour of the city and the surrounding area. Vianen still reverberates with the spirit of the Brederodes. Much beauty and many enchantments—such as the beautiful medieval city hall with its collection of historical paintings, the prison, and the city walls—still exist. The mayor brought us to the vaulted cellars where, by candlelight, the conspirators, the Orange supporters and the Brederodes, came together to discuss the contents of pamphlets that were widely distributed and made available through the clandestine print shop of the Brederodes during the resistance against Spain.

Of the proud castle of the Brederodes, only a solitary small gate remains. The States of Holland had it demolished.

Around 1700, there lived a family member of the Lippes, Countess Van Limburg Stirum; she reached the age of ninety. The Van Noorles knew her and valued her stately appearance.

Our next visit concerned the Grote Kerk (*the Big Church*), which was tastefully restored after WWII. The purpose was to visit the funeral vault of the family, which caused some difficulties. The entrance was blocked by one of the three organs proudly owned by the church, and our forefathers were transferred, sometime later, to the cemetery.

Instead of the family funeral vault, we descended into the funeral vault of the Brederodes in which at least twenty-four members were interned. There we saw the skull of Walraven, who, in 1417, died in a fight with Jan van Arkel. The skull showed a deep cut above the forehead and a cut on one of the sides. It was the custom to knock an opponent unconscious with a sword strike and then hit him with a second strike when he was lying on the ground. Both Walraven and Jan van Arkel succumbed. The skull of Floris V (in Rijnsburg) shows the same injuries.

From there, the journey continued to Monikkenhof. Half of an iron gate, with a cast-iron sign of the house's name that was missing a few letters and lying on the side of a ditch, was the only remaining remnant of our forefather's house. The rest was a meadow in which the contours of the foundation were vaguely visible. Next to it is still the majestic entrance to the gentleman farmhouse with an unimpaired Bentzbergh sign. It belonged to the family Bentz van den Bergh of Vianen.

We had a little more luck at Heicop. Floris van Hall bought this manor at the end of the eighteenth century and used the beautiful house for hunting parties. Sadly, the house itself was swallowed up by the pastures, but the courthouse, *Regthuis,* is still standing. In the small vestibule, where weekly meetings of the city council are still held today, hangs a painting of Huis Heicop by Adriaan van Hall. One can see the two stone pillars that are now across the street and in the garden of the church. The lord of the manor had the *collatierecht*, which gave him the right to appoint ministers. The last lord of the manor, F. A. van Hall, Esq. (1838–1929), occasionally had the naughty pleasure of burdening this orthodox community with a liberal minister.

We drove along prosperous farms and orchards, and Mayor Pellikaan told us about the flood disasters that plagued this beautiful countryside in previous centuries. From these disasters arose the term "spade stitch due to foreclosure" (*spadesteek wegens verponding*). This spade stitch occurred in those days more often than not. After a flood, the taxes were raised to pay for the restoration of the dikes, while the farmer's income had dried up due to the flood and the farmland was still underwater. When the farmer did not see any way out to pay his taxes, he stuck his spade in the ground in front of his house. The first one who pulled out the spade took on the responsibility to pay the overdue taxes and became the owner of the homestead. Unscrupulous people with ready money saw this as a chance to expand their landholdings.

We were alarmed when we heard this news as we had seen the long list of properties that Floris left behind. To our relief, the mayor assured us that there was no evidence that the family participated in these misbehaviors.

With this, we end our investigation of the origins of the family. The hors d'oeuvres have been served, and now we come to the first course on the menu of these remembrances: the life of Maurits Cornelis, the fifth child of Floris and the founding father of the Amsterdam Van Halls.

THE PATRIARCH OF THE AMSTERDAM VAN HALLS

MAURITS CORNELIS VAN HALL, 1768–1858

His godfather was Maurits Cornelis de Waal van Lexmond, Lord of Lexmond, Agthoven, and Nederfelt. Thus did the name Maurits Cornelis enter the family, which in the following generations, due to overuse, caused much confusion.

Maurits had a blissful youth, and his family was close-knit. The schooling in Vianen could not offer much, so when he was eleven years old, he was sent to Vicar Claeszen in Leerdam to study Greek and Latin.

Leerdam does not lie far from Vianen; further, the mother of Maurits had family living there. Her brother Johan van Noorle occupied in Leerdam a number of positions among which were steward of the Dukely Dominions of Leerdam and Acquoy (*Rentmeester van de Grafelijke Domeinen van Leerdam en Acquoy*) and mayor of Leerdam, and he was also on the Board of the Dikes in the Collegium of five Gentlemen Lands (*Hoogdijkheemraad in het Collegie der vijf Heeren Landen wegens ter Leede*). He was married to Margaretha van der Does, daughter of a General Van der Does. She lost with one stroke a great part of her family. Her parents died at the same time in Batavia, Indonesia, and her two sisters drowned on the return voyage close to the Cape of Good Hope.

When Maurits was fourteen, he went to Utrecht to study law. He connected with a number of friends who were taught by a colonel, Gordon, in military strategies. Actually, Maurits wanted to pursue a career in the military and drop the study of law. With a powerful build that was as strong as an ox, he admired body strength. This was evident in a note in his diary about a walk with the famous professor Bellamy to the Bilt. On this occasion, Maurits, in the inn and with one hand, squeezed a tin tankard full of beer so hard that the beer splashed onto the ceiling of the room where they were. It splashed so much that hardly a drop of beer was left in the tankard.

Father Floris did not want to hear of a military career and made short shrift of that. He sent Maurits to the university in Leiden. In 1787, he spent his summer vacation at home. He brought his books along from Leiden to write his doctoral thesis. Not much work was accomplished as it was too turbulent in the land of Vianen.

Here, three centuries ago is where it all started.
The watermill on the Klingelbeek, below Oosterbeek, as it appeared in 1809.
drawing by B. Kerkhoff, County Museum of Arnhem.

The castle of the Brederode's in Vianen around 1640.

The rural gateway in Vianen around 1800. Here the rebellious
son of a farmer from Meerkerk was imprisoned, set secretly
free by the daughter of the jail keeper late at night.

Willem V, the stadtholder prince, was relieved of his duties by the regents, and his wife, Princess Wilhelmina, was assaulted at the Goejanverwellesluis. The followers of the Orange (*Oranje*) family did not take to that, and time and time again, riots erupted.

One day, Maurits was allowed to go to Meerkerk, a small village to the west of Vianen, where a gang of rebellious farmers raised an orange flag in the church tower during the horse market. Vader Floris, in his function as substitute steward, took command. The riot was suppressed, and the leaders were imprisoned in the prison of Vianen. The daughter of the prison warden secretly let them loose that night, but that was not taken too seriously. Among them was a farmer's handsome son.

Of more interest was the campaign to Leerdam. On horseback, he accompanied his father to conquer that little city—"*dat stedeke te vermeesteren.*" It could evidently not handle the comparison with the proud Vianen. Mayor Knijff and the lay judge De Man were, under guard, brought back to Vianen and imprisoned.

Later that summer, a major threat developed. The King of Prussia decided to come to the aid of his maligned sister with an army. On 16 September 1787, the Prussians approached from the direction of Leerdam.

The Dutch army consisted of the cavalry of the regiment Van Tuyll, a part of the Gelderland brigade under the command of Citizen-Captain Daendels, and a part of the regiment Van Handenbroek,[1] the latter of which Maurits joined as a volunteer. With another volunteer named Heimeriks, he had to guard a broken bridge over the canal that separated Boeicop and Bolgarije.

And our nineteen-year-old man became frightened when the Prussian cavalry on the other side of the canal opened fire with carbines and pistols, while he only had a blunderbuss. He wanted to flee, but the fearless Heimeriks warned him that thereupon, a bullet would be awaiting him. Luckily, a horseman appeared from Van Tuyll at the eleventh hour with the command to retreat to the farmhouse *Het Pannehuis*, which is somewhat closer to Vianen.

After arriving in record time, he found a distraught colonel who, at the urging of the troops, was relieved of his command. Daendels took over the command and formed a defensive square and decided to retreat. The volunteers were discharged.

Maurits hurried home, where his father, Floris, together with his brother Adriaan, were busy with loading valuables and important papers into a farm

---

[1]   There was no Van Hardenbroek with the regiment because they favored the Orange family. Lodewijk Willem Adolph Baron van Hardenbroek followed Prince Willem V to England and lived on the Isle of Wight with other exiles. In later years, he distinguished himself in the battle against Napoleon.

wagon. His mother and sister had earlier fled to Amsterdam. Armed with two loaded muskets and the blunderbuss, the group, as fast as possible, made their way to the ferryboat over the river Lek. There was a throng of military men, and the colonel initially forbade the ferryman to load the farm wagon. The ferryman owed so much to Father Floris that he refused to cross without the farm wagon. After some squabbling, the colonel gave in. It was high time he did so because just after the ferry pushed off the shore, the Prussian cavalry galloped over the Hagensteinse Dijk, shooting away.

After arriving on the other side, they heard that Utrecht had surrendered, and thus the voyage continued as they followed a long row of refugees around IJsselstein and along a detour to Nieuwendijk. Time and again they were harassed by "Orange above All" people, and occasionally they had to show their loaded weapons. The inns along the way were full of warriors with "all sorts of coats of arms." Nevertheless, in the country estate of Mr. Ludens along the river Vecht, they found food and a moment of rest.

On 17 September, the group arrived late in the evening in Amsterdam and started walking to the house of Adriaan Teyler van Hall on the Herengracht, across from the Bergstraat. This Adriaan had already lived in Amsterdam for a couple of years and had added the name of his wife, Teyler, to his own.

Adriaan took Maurits forthwith to the Fatherland Society (*Vaderlandsche Sociëteit*) in the Kalverstraat, a club of patriots with the nickname of "*Keezen.*" Here Maurits reported on the events; the fall of Utrecht was not known yet in Amsterdam, and this news spread like wildfire throughout the city. It reached the ears of the Defense Group meeting at the Doelen Hotel. Maurits was arrested at the club and brought to the Defense Group. He was accused of spreading false rumors and agitating unrest.

He furiously exploded and said, *"I offer myself as a hostage until you see for yourself I am speaking the truth. Rather, instead, do something to chase away the enemy."*

The Amsterdam magistrates set him free and did nothing about the war. In October, the Prussians occupied the city.

Maurits moved in with his uncle, Herman van Noorle, who lived on the Singel next to the Utrecht Ferry, and devoted himself further to his studies.

We have now witnessed the third migration of the family under dramatic though also comical circumstances. With the annexation of Vianen by Holland around the corner, it was evident that not much honor could be gotten in that city. Maurits thus decided to settle in Amsterdam.

In 1788, he was registered there as a lawyer. Remarkably, the first case he had to handle concerned an inheritance squabble of a farmer in Lexmond. The farmer found himself on 19 September 1787 near Monnikenhof, the parental house of Maurits. When he saw the Prussian hussars coming at him, he quickly wrote his will in his pocket book, leaving everything to his wife. He was killed, and different heirs disputed the legality of the will. Maurits brought the case to a good end.

The following year, in 1789, he got engaged to Elisabeth Klinkhamer, the daughter of Jacob Klinkhamer, Esq., a lawyer in Amsterdam and a bailiff of Ilpendam. Jacob was friends with Mr. A. Dedel. Because Mr. Dedel was the ruler of professions (*ambachtsheer*) of the newer Amstel, he could, together with Klinkhamer, convince the notary to hand over his duties to Maurits. This happened according to the good old custom among the regents to make a marriage happen sooner. And so they already could marry the next year. In 1803, his father-in-law made himself useful and bought from the bookstore Daetselaar in Gorinchem the famous chest in which Hugo the Great later was able to escape from Loevenstein. This chest is now in the Rijksmuseum.

Mayor Rendorp was also kindly disposed to him; he received from him the task to settle the war damages that occurred during the occupation of the Prussians. In the meantime, his law practice steadily prospered. Among the young lawyers he especially became friends with are R. J. Schimmelpenninck, J. Bondt, and C. J. Elout.

In the beginning, there were troubles in principle due to the animosity of J. W. van de Poll, Esq., the presiding lay judge. Van de Poll, a descendant of the famous mayoral dynasty of that name, viewed the youthful, aggressive patriot as an interloper and a danger to the existing order. He did not let an opportunity to work against him or insult him pass. The things Van de Poll had done against him slowly became the talk of the day. This started to aggravate a great uncle of Maurits, Christiaan van Noorle, so much that he decided to put an end to this.

He proceeded as follows. He invited Van de Poll and Maurits to his country house, Het Huis te Capelle, which was situated between Muiden and Wezep, to have an extended drink (*eenen roes*). The binge lasted two days and three nights. For poor Maurits, this was an awful torment because until that moment, he had been free of alcohol. In his daybook, he momentarily moved to Latin and wrote, "Viri probi et qui praeclarae lariae honore praefulgebunt." Loosely translated, it means, "The respectable men shall excel through a graceful and magnificent wreath of rubbish." Thus it did not mean a laurel wreath! The word *laria* does not exist in Latin, although it was used in that sense by, among others, the author Betje Wolff.

The result was surprising. From that moment on, Van de Poll and Maurits became the best of friends.

Maurits linked up with the Amsterdam patriots, and he landed in good company. The regime had gotten so corrupt that many young patricians—such as Van Lennep, Dedel, and Roell—also became patriots. The Fatherland Society (*Vaderlandsche Sociëteit*), the customary meeting place, was outlawed at the end of 1789, and an order was issued to sell the building immediately. Through some stooges, the members bought the building themselves, and after a while, under the bogus name Literary Society "Doctrina et Amicitia"—*Groote Club*, on that spot arose a much bigger clubhouse. The cornerstone, placed by Jan Hendrik Rauwenhoff, is in the front house of the club, and the memorial stone of the Fatherland Society has been placed on a wall of the billiards hall and can still be viewed today in the Groote Club—"Doctrina et Amicitia." The reading hall could only be accessed through a high and steep staircase, and we read in one of the annual reports that once they arrived upstairs, the members were wont to lie down and fall asleep—a phenomenon one can still observe today, although the steep staircase has disappeared and been replaced by an elevator.

Maurits belonged to the moderate patriots, and he was fiercely opposed to the pro-French elements among them. He did not think the time was ripe for an upheaval and definitely did not want one that needed the help of the French. When one of the secret conspiracies was discovered, Uncle Valkenburg and Dr. Krayenhoff were left in mortal danger, and Maurits helped them escape. A servant of his father brought them in a carriage to Vianen via Gorinchem. In Monnikenhof, they remained hidden for a while. For extra assurance, Father Floris gave them a Vianen safe conduct.

During this period, the regents advised the inhabitants to wear orange to prevent their being accosted in the streets. Maurits was more than put off by this; he said that they more appropriately should have issued a ruling because he then naturally would have worn orange. He had, after all, a great respect for the law. Since it was only a suggestion, he flatly refused. The consequence of this is that on an afternoon at the Dam, he got attacked and beat up by a throng. He fled to the bookstore Dronsberg, where a couple of men of the Swiss Guard came to rescue him.

We leave Maurits momentarily to see how his older brother, Rev. Herman van Hall, is fairing. He was, in 1785, appointed by A. Ph. Baron van der Capellen as the preacher in his Blessed Berkenwoude. The family Van der Capellen stood in the front ranks of the patriots.

When Baron Van der Capellen died in 1788, the patriotic Reverend Van Hall delivered a fierce eulogy. It was a very hazardous task—"*een uiterst hagchelijke taak*"—but luckily, it was without bad repercussions for him.

The deceased was a cousin of the great Jan Dereck van der Capellen, the undisputed leader of the patriots. He died in 1784 from symptoms of poisoning shortly after opening a letter sent by a political opponent. This was, according to a legend in his family, a "poison letter" that people sent to others occasionally in earlier times. The letter would contain such a strong poison that an unsuspecting victim had no chance.

We decided that a thorough, in-depth investigation was necessary as the name of the author was known to us and we are convinced that she did not do this. First of all, we were reassured about the circumstances in that even modern science, currently does not know of a poison with such dreadful consequences. We have come to the conclusion that the text of the letter was the cause of death; it caused a heart attack or a stroke. The letter was loaded with blame and accusation directed at Jan Dereck. We felt justified in our opinion when we found out that after WWII, a number of tax assessments covering instant demands (*heffing Ineens*) and capital gains (*vermogensaanwas*) were sent out. A few wealthy Dutchmen, sitting behind their desks, were found dead with opened envelopes and assessment notices in their hands that were stiffened by rigor mortis. The cause of death? Each died after reading the amount of their particular assessment. Secretary of State for Finance A. F. van Hall had also been accused of having gotten rid of a political opponent through a poisoned letter. The cause of death? The opening of the assessment for an obligatory loan in 1844 with the threat that the banking secrecy would be dissolved if it failed. For more complete certainty, we turned to Squire F. J. E. van Lennep, the author of *De Hattekamp*, as rumors had reached us that Jacob van Lennep knew more about this type of poison letter. This turned out not to be the case, and Mr. van Lennep gave us the following comment: "Sadly, I also fail in this area of poison!"

In his book *Wandelingen door Rome* (*Walking through Rome*), Dutch author Godfried Bomans devoted a chapter to Jan Dereck van der Capellen. On one of his walks, he discovered a monumental group of sculptures dedicated to his memory; sadly, the group never made its way to Holland. Why don't some enterprising Dutchmen join together to get the sculptures to Zwolle and give Jan Dereck the place he deserves there?

In 1795, the upheaval occurred. The French army invaded Holland, and was followed by a couple of thousand patriots who had gone into exile in France.

There was no fighting in Amsterdam. While on the Dam, a few French soldiers stood guard. The town council came together in its last meeting to turn over the reign to the provisional representatives of the people of Amsterdam. Somewhat saddened though unhindered, the members of the town council returned home. It was over for the once-so-glorious Republic of the Seven Provinces (*Republiek der Zeven Provincien*).

The first order of business of the new rulers was to maintain order. They created the Commission of Justice; among them were R. J. Schimmelpenninck and J. Sinderam, both good friends of Maurits. It was difficult to find a candidate for the position of city prosecutor (*stadsprocureur*)—a combination of a public prosecutor and chief superintendant of the police (*schout*). It was a function that was not appealing to an Amsterdam-born person. The eye fell on Maurits, who was more of an outsider. He declined, noting his inexperience and youthful age (twenty-six years); however, he received shortly afterward his appointment with the message that if he still refused, he would be held responsible for any riots and disturbances and would be punished for them.

He begrudgingly started work. In November 1795, trouble erupted. The impoverished masses (*gepeupel*) wanted, along the French example, to guillotine a number of regents and rob their houses. To them, all Orange-minded civil servants needed to be locked up. He could apply to his heart's content the military-strategy lessons he learned in Utrecht.

In the middle of the night, the impoverished masses acquired the keys to the city gates. These were, every night, put into a chest in the room of the armed guard in the city hall. The armed guards were overpowered. Nobody could enter or exit the city now.

Maurits was still lying in bed when he heard the alarming news. He alerted a troop of city soldiers and a company of citizen gunners under the command of Captain J. Tideman. He himself hurried to the city hall and forced himself into the guardroom that was occupied by the opponents. Initially, he tried to reason with them, but when they physically attacked him, he had to defend himself with his sword. It was one of the most dangerous situations in his life. Neither of the parties gave in, and it took a while before he heard the drums and help appeared. With great difficulty, he reestablished order in the city. While he addressed the rebellious populace, he placed gunners on both sides of the city hall. The burning wicks were brought closer, and with the threat of gunfire, the mob retreated.

A citizen of Amsterdam, Mr. W. Scharff, was murdered that night in the Kalverstraat, and Maurits had the perpetrators arrested. Late one evening, their supporters had themselves announced as the representatives of a district assembly to Maurits. Among them was a bookseller, W. Holtrop (who later would be the chief superintendant of the police). Maurits received the group in the big side room of his house, De Hardebollen, on the Herengracht. With swearing and threats, they demanded the immediate release of the prisoners. He explained why he could not do this, and when they did not want to leave, he pulled out of his desk (*secretaire*) two pistols (although they were unloaded) and marched them out of his house. Once they were outside and on the canal, he heard one of them say, "He is a smart guy, and he sure f———d us."

He was able to protect ex-mayors Beels, d'Orville, Elias, and Dedel from a furious crowd who wanted to snatch them out of their homes. It was a good opportunity for him to repay his old debt to Dedel. He was on the run night and day, his sword more often in his hand than in its scabbard.[2]

If a prisoner did not want to confess, the "Sharp-Edged Examination" would be applied. In other words, the prisoner would get the rack. But generally, the threat of the rack was sufficient enough to reveal the truth!

Maurits detested the death penalty. He only used it a few times, and even those times were not for political reasons but for crimes. This was the case of Leendert van der Willigen, who had to climb onto the gallows on the Dam for making counterfeit two and a half guilder coins from Zeeland.

A scandal pamphlet, *The Political Lightning* (*De Politieke Blixem*), was published, which caused many acts of violence. The editor was a certain Redelinkhuyzen. In his later years, he became remorseful, and shortly before his death, he, through a friend, asked Maurits if he could forgive him. Redelinkhuyzen had done much wrong.

Through the ages, during turbulent times, the Jews were always persecuted. This was, for Redelinkhuyzen, a highly popular subject. Maurits wrote in his daybook about how disgusted he was with these persecutions and he spoke with just pride of not only how he, as a city prosecutor, combated this but also How he once personally intervened in the persecutions.

Late one afternoon in September 1795, he walked across the Dam and saw to his dismay that an elderly Jew, who for years had a stand next to the Nieuwe Kerk, was being brutally beaten up by a certain Christoffel Hunnemeyer. The man was lying on the ground and bleeding profusely. Maurits imprudently did not have the usual attendant from the Ministry of Justice with him. He rushed over and asked Hunnemeyer what the reason for the mistreatment was. Hunnemeyer said, "It just is a damn Jew." Maurits grabbed the man, and after an intense fight, he, together with a passing guard, succeeded in bringing the

---

[2] Even during this turbulent period, he still found the time to successfully defend an accused man who he thought did not deserve the death sentence. A certain Herman Alfkens had killed two of his children just outside of Amsterdam on the so-called Lange Bleekerspad. When the turn came for his third child, he lost his courage. He was arrested. According to his neighbors, Alfkens was always a warm and loving father. Poverty and perilous circumstances brought him to this awful deed. He believed that once they were dead, he and his children would lead a better life in heaven and that God would forgive him for this act. Maurits, the case's prosecutor, presented a plea that took many hours—the longest address he ever made in court. In deviation of the prevailing opinions, he argued that Alfkens was guilty of the act but not the crime. He stated that Alfkens was unstable and acted in a moment of insanity. He believed that a different standard had to be applied in this case. He said that the accused did not deserve the death penalty but incarceration. The verdict was fifty years' imprisonment.

handcuffed man to the city hall. It so happened that the judges were in court, and justice was handed down instantly.

The villain was shortly placed on the scaffold on the Dam (that apparently was permanently placed there) with a sign around his neck on which was written "Molester of his fellow human being [*Mishandelaar van zijn evenmensch*]." In front of the flocking crowd, he was seriously whipped, and then he was locked up for six years in the Planing House, *het Rasphuis*. This was quick justice, and we can imagine that other miscreants who witnessed this took the punishment to heart. The Rasphuis was not a pleasant prison and was intended for men who had to plane certain different woods to make them ready for painting. The Spinning House, *Spinhuis*, was reserved for women who had to spin.

To the great annoyance of Maurits, in May of the following year, Hunnemeyer escaped when the masses stormed the jail and threw open its doors to let out all the prisoners who Maurits, with so much difficulty and trouble, had locked up. He retrieved a large number, but Hunnemeyer was not among them. Apparently, one encounter with the prosecutor was enough.[3]

Another time, Maurits noticed how a mob pursued and threatened a merchant and banker, Mr. Pieter Muilman, returning from the stock exchange. Mr. Muilman started running and fled into the Kalverstraat; next to the St. Luciensteeg, the mob got ahold of him and started beating him up. Maurits was again alone—he had already sent his servants home; thus he quickly walked to the Groote Club—*Sociëteit "Doctrina et Amicitia"*—and asked the members there to help him free the victim. Hastily they grabbed their weapons and followed Maurits on foot. After a heavy fight at which solid punches were exchanged, they were able to carry the seriously wounded Muilman into a cake bakery.

When one sees the current members of the Groote Club sitting behind the windows, the involuntary question of whether they could rise to a similar occasion comes up. This has been confirmed. During the Second World War, many occupied high positions in the resistance, and some paid the ultimate price.

The unpleasant profession of city prosecutor claimed high demands, and Maurits slowly but surely had enough. The urge to institute a reign of terror

---

[3]   Some examples of convictions in 1795:
1 April: Mulders (Geurt)—sentenced to a heavy whipping on the scaffold, confined for five years in Rasphuis, and then banned from Holland for revolutionary activities.
1 April: Praag (Jannetje van)—sentenced to a whipping on the scaffold, confined for five years in Spinhuis, and then banned from Holland for calling out "Hurray for Orange [*Oranje Boven*]."
6 April: Schenk (Anthony)—two years in Rasphuis due to spreading false rumors.

became stronger, but he did not always get the right amount of backing from the city council.

Once in a while, he was forced by the Commission of Justice to imprison people who, according to him, did not belong there. That was the case for Lieutenant-Admiral Van Kinsbergen. Maurits went to the prison room in the city hall to personally offer his excuses for the injustice that had befallen him and tried his best to free him. This was the beginning of a lifelong, close relationship.[4]

Below we quote a passage from his day journal that perfectly reflects the situation at that time in Amsterdam. He did not write with the *I* form but described himself using *he* or *prosecutor.*

> *On Tuesday, the 10th of May 1796, his parents during this time located in Amsterdam with a large part of His family at His house for the mid day meal, he received the confirmation that the earlier received message that a large number of armed and "Freedom" shouting Mutineers who had their eye on not only the City Government and the dismissal of the Gunners, but also work on the dismissal of the prisoners Mozeman, Swieter and Kloosterman, and immediately compel with violence the Board of the So-called Emotional Orange Civil Servants* [Eemotie der Zogenaamde Oranje-Ambtenaren] *to disband. His Parents, Blood and Married Kin leaving hastily behind, he made his way to the City Hall where the City Council was meeting before which an ever growing force of armed citizens, under the command of Commander G. H. de Wilde, was assembled. Arriving at City Hall he found the Committee on Vigilance* [Committé van Waakzaamheid] *in session, with the earlier mentioned Commandant present. Of the criminal purpose of the gunners who were let go and their relationship with the armed citizens, he made the Committee aware of the situation and urged the Commandant to now use the force before it was too late, to either control the rebellious crowd or disperse them.*

> *Soon he noticed that the Commandant was in league with the rebels and started a vehement exchange and accused him outright of a weak and cowardly conduct. De Wilde, hereupon put his hand on his sword and said "Citizen Prosecutor do you know I have a sword?" upon*

---

[4]   Simultaneously with Van Kinsbergen, the fiscal counsel of the navy, J. C. van der Hoop was locked up. Maurits regarded them as the bearers of the highest traditions of the navy and as people who should not be entangled in the troubles of the revolution.

which instantly the Prosecutor said "I have a sword just like you, Citizen Commandant, and am willing to use it." Upon which De Wilde shut up, while the roar on the Dam kept growing.

After a while it became apparent that the primary goal of the rebellious crowd was the setting free of Mozeman, Swieter and Kloosterman from the City Jail—"Stede Boeyen"—and Hunnemeijer from the "Rasphuis" which, if necessary, would be accomplished with violence, he with his co-committee members went to the Hearing Chamber and instructed the Warden to follow only His orders. After he subsequently put his wife somewhat at ease and relayed the uncertainty of the time of his return home, he departed again for City Hall and with only one Court servant went to the Council Chamber, which he with difficulty and life-threatening effort through an entangled and mixed crowd of armed rifle men and former Gunners, entered; and heard the Chamber filled with those who had pushed in with their rebellious shouting and that the setting free of the stated prisoners was not a priority, but now insisted on the most awful demands. Having approached the location of Mr. A. Vereul, President of the Council, he found, at the same time that he noticed, the Magistrate-person in his confusion tearing up the publication through which the Gunners were let go, in pieces and the remnants lying around the floor. Shortly he was asked by the confused Magistrate to free the aforementioned prisoners, which he answered with "If the Council was authorized to do so by the Provincial Board of Holland?" and then he himself answered "No" and refused in a strong voice that that was contrary to his oath. The same question was posed to the co-committee members Van Ommeren and Glimmer by the President and like himself gave the same answer; upon which the President gave the order to unlock the prison and let the aforementioned prisoners free. During all this he was in mortal danger, threatened with murder and robbery and at one point one of the rebels wanted to throw him out the window of the Council Chamber.

The little bridge near Bolgerije, between Vianen and Hagelstein, where young
Maurits van Hall with his musket tried to stop the Prussians.

The rural Gateway and the big church in Vianen

The gateway from the dykes to Hattem around 1900

The conquest of Hattem by Van Spengler over Daendels in 1786

The battle near Bergen, Province of North Holland on 19 September, 1799.
Collectie Atlas van Stolk

Illustration of Adriaan Teyler van Hall and
Engel van de Stadt's pirate ship in battle.

With difficulty and mortal danger and under the command of Surgeon Major of the City Citizen Cavalry, C. Vissen, he found himself leaving the Council Chambers around two o'clock in the morning with his co-council members, which most of the co-members already had left, on his way home. Once arriving in the Leliestraat and noticing a sound behind him, he saw a man with a big knife in his hand. Luckily he discovered in him an acquaintance, the Jeweler Kool, who without wanting to be noticed was following him to protect him. Arriving at his home, he immediately notified the members of the Committee to gather at his house at seven the next morning, the 11th of May. All appeared and saw him give them a written report.[5] Receiving this with much thanks it was decided 1) that as one body they would go the City Council to ask them "if they thought they had enough power to support the Court of Justice in its maintenance of its duty" 2) to appoint a Commission with as goal to go to The Hague "to ask the Provincial Council of Holland to reaffirm the role and duties of the Prosecutor of the Municipality and all the implications." To this end he, as well as the Gentlemen Van Ommeren, Burley Glimmer and the Secretary of the Committee J. C. de Bordes were appointed.

Subsequently, he with all the Members went to the City Council, who not feeling safe in City Hall had gone to the Doelen on the Garnalenmarkt, and received to his question the following answer "that the Council had no power due to the previous happenings, and was not able to act ACTIVELY, and decided to just do the regular work, and in everything else conduct itself PASSIVELY." In the speech he gave on this occasion, he mentioned that the riflemen were fellow-revolutionaries, which one of the Members of the Council held against him.

The same day he, together with the Commission, departed for The Hague [Gravenhage] and arrived there at ten o'clock in the evening. During this trip a speech was composed and directed at the Provincial Council. He, together with his fellow commission members, the following afternoon at three o'clock were admitted to this Council where he delivered his elaborate Account and Secretary de Bordes presented them with the written Report. This Address was favorably

---

5   This report is found on page 78 of *Minutes of the Committee of Justice.* The whole report was written and composed by Mr. Glimmer during the middle of the revolt and in the council chambers. A better example of fearlessness and courage, one will rarely see.

absorbed and accepted with evident appreciation for the way the Court of Justice had behaved; he and his co-commission members forthwith departed to Amsterdam, still on 12 May, 1795, and gave, with his co-commissioners, an Account of what they had accomplished.

Upon their return they saw some discharged gunners standing guard at the Haarlemmerpoort. Their carriage halted by them and tempestuously questioned if they came from The Hague, which was answered "Yes" by the Prosecutor of the Municipality, adding "that the troops sent to re-establish order were already under way," which upset the Questioners who let the carriage pass.

During their absence he had His Spouse with both of His young Sons, Floris Adriaan and Adriaan, in addition to his servants, except a trustworthy Valet[6] leave his house which was threatened with plunder, the care of which he delegated to the aforementioned Valet, the Coachman of His Father-In-Law, Klinkhamer, and two of his most courageous and trustworthy Servants of the Justice Ministry all armed with various guns and other weapons. Aside from some disturbances nothing happened during His absence. The Perpetrators were exhausted and were afraid of the future, while the cowardly City Council blaming each other, was ashamed.

The previously mentioned prisoners were set free on the night of 10 to 11 May on the order by the President of the Council, with the Members den Beer Portugael and Pontoi assuring him when they saw him waver that "You have nothing to worry about because the Council has decided" and Council Member Meynst let himself be used too.

When after a couple of weeks peace had returned to Amsterdam and the Department of Justice was functioning again, he caught the freed prisoners who thought they could stay without penalty in the city and charged them again. This and his determined refusal to renounce his

---

6   He was indebted to the valet for the well-being of his oldest son (Floris Adriaan, the future secretary of state). In 1799, in Gravenhage and during a sham battle in the Haagsche Bos, Floris Adriaan was knocked over by artillery horses, and the valet protected him with his own body, the act causing him serious injuries. For this courage and care, he was able to arrange for this faithful servant the position of courier in the Ministry of Finances.

oath and duty, and conduct himself according to "arbitrium popularis aurea," led to his removal of his position on 15 March, 1798.

About the release of Hunnemeyer, De Bosch Kemper said in the preface of the third part of the essay of his father, "The council had, in spite of the fearless courage of Maurits's opposition against the release, set the prisoners free."

On 15 March 1798, the States Commission dismissed Maurits as city prosecutor of the City of Amsterdam. This occurred in a stately manner in the ships chamber of the city hall. After coming home, he handed his sword and his hat à la française to his servant and exchanged them for a round hat and a cane. Thus armed, he traversed in a defiant manner through the poorer sections of the city. His first steps were directed to the Jewish quarter, where great anxiety reigned now that Hunnemeyer and other rogues were released from prison and new acts of violence would occur. His dismissal did not last long because after General Daendels returned from a secret mission to Paris, he restored order, and Maurits resumed his functions as city prosecutor.

The reader must permit us to let Maurits tell the events in his own words; also, in this paragraph, he used *prosecutor* or *he* to describe himself. The city commission consisted of P. R. Pieterse; J. Romswinkel, Esq.; D. Pompeira; and J. A. Bode.

P. R. Pieterse, pale and flustered, read with an emotional voice the legal ground for the dismissal of the Prosecutor of the Municipality and the Members of the Commission of Justice from their respective functions. The content of this speech is reported in its entirety in the Proceedings of the Committee of Justice and it is therefore strange in that it openly declares that this dismissal was based on no other reasons than the rebellious events on January 22, 1798, although it was well known that the bold and irrefutable Address of 7 February 1798 of the outgoing regime had concluded this "ab erato." The Prosecutor of the Municipality and the Justice Department of which he was the head, dared to assert:

That no Sovereign Meeting, even including the Board of the Provinces of Holland, had the power to nullify any case pending in court;

And not afraid, he reminded the Reconstituted Meeting of the well known reference of Cicero translated as follows:

"In corrupt states in which all affairs are hopeless, the disastrous ultimately is the norm, where crooks are acquitted, where sentences are

revoked and the prisoners are set free. If all these events happen, there will be nobody who notices that the community is being destroyed."

They had, moreover, in their indignation dared to compare the conduct of the Provincial Board with the rules of the Emperors of Rome who were given the name of tyrants and even those that were dictated by the Spanish Philips; by the first mentioned L 7, Cod. De precibus Imp. Off. and L 6 Cod. Si Contra Jus and by the latter in the renowned Religious Ordinance practiced for over two centuries by the Criminal Justice in the Netherlands. The previously reported legal ground was answered by M. C. van Hall, Esq., for himself as well as his countrymen, in the following manner:

"Citizens! With a clear conscience we entered this Chamber of Justice when we, were given our positions by those who had received the power from the Citizens, we now, with a clear conscience, leave this place on Your orders. This conscience assures us that whatever fate lies ahead for the Fatherland or us, we will never stop loving the Fatherland!"

With this they left the Justice Chambers in the same order upon which they had entered and left City Hall to be greeted, with a moving silence, by a significant crowd of Citizens.

Coming home he wholeheartedly embraced his wife and children, gave his sword and hat "à la Francaise" to his faithful servant, while his faithful Elisabeth Christina cried with happiness and thanked God, and after a little while, went out that late afternoon and evening to assess how the community viewed him. To that end he walked in black clothes—as usual—with a round hat on and a small cane in his hand, alone and unaccompanied, he went into that part of the city where the lower classes lived. Handsome, most likely due to his posture and firm walk, he noticed unmistakably the respect given him and no one bore him ill will. In particular this first became evident in the Jewish Quarter; coming home from City Hall he let it be known that that evening he would direct his walk there. He aimed his walk therefore in that direction. Barely out of the Hoogstraat and arriving on the Joden Breestraat, he noticed a number of Jews announcing his arrival to the south side of the street, hurrying and with for him unintelligible sounds. Walking slowly and stately in the middle of the street, he was greeted wholeheartedly and with distinction by the rich and the poor and more than once he heard the words "His name is great in Israel" and so with emotion he left the so-called Jewish Quarter and appeared on the Kattenburg and went from there along the periphery to Bikkers Eiland and from there along various streets in the neighborhood of the Brouwersgracht, home where his wife more than rejoiced on his return, from his not very safe walk. He spent the night of 15 to 16 March, 1798 free of worries and complete rest, something he had not had in a long time. Barely awake and in a condition to receive someone, a group of the best citizens of the city, with different views on how the city should be run, announced themselves to wish him the best. One of them, Mr. S. Gildenmeester, after asking how much the annual salary was for the Prosecutor of the Municipality, offered him, although with great sensitivity, to pay him the remainder of his salary until he would not need it anymore. With deep gratitude for so much sympathy, he declined this generous offer, which he would not have done if fate had made it necessary.

He was replaced as Prosecutor of the Municipality by Mr. den Beer Poortugael.

The three months, after his release of his position, he spent in the country, at Monnikenhof close to Vianen, at Heikop[7] and at Ilpendam with his parents and parents-in-law and occupied himself mostly giving advice as a lawyer and formulating many opinions, none of which were meant for official publication. He abstained, as many famous Jurists,[8] to appear before the Courts, which was composed in such a way that he would feel ashamed of himself to present a case. One talked about and it was the truth that a Madam was indicted on maintaining underage girls, but she claimed to run a proper house plying her trade and to prove it she called on one of the Judges who was part of the trial saying "Citizen B knows this, as he is a daily visitor to my house."

In this manner the 12ᵗʰ of June, 1798 approached after General Daendels, using a good carriage, returned on the 10ᵗʰ of that month from his secret mission to Paris and overthrew, with the support of the

---

7   *It is primarily here that he, then and later, learned about estate management—a healthy, welcome reprieve from his previous work. The stay there had had a lasting impression on him and his children, especially H. C. van Hall, who discovered botany and found through it his profession as professor of agriculture and estate management.*

8   *Among these were, above all, Sinderarm, Farjon, Bondt, and R. J. Schimmelpenninck.*

whole population, the current regime which had been established with much violence on 22 January. And business as usual was allowed to return to the great relief of the peaceful and order minded Dutch people.

The result was the reinstatement of the Prosecutor of the Municipality and the Members of the Justice Committee in their positions from which they had been removed on 15 March. This happened without letting of blood or resistance and already on 13 June 1798 with the blessing of the citizens they could resume their positions they had had to leave.

In those years, he still found the time for literature and religious practice. He even wrote six songs, which were included in the collection of poems of C. de Vries and C. Sepp Jansz. They were numbers 6, 16, 47, 84, 97, and 122, and some of their titles were the following: "The Comfort of the Evening Meal [*De vertroosting des Avondmaals*]," "God All Knowing [*God Alwetend*]," "Jesus Betrayed by Petrus [*Jezus verloochend door Petrus*]," and "Paean to Jesus the Savior [*Lofzang aan Jezus de Verlosser*]."

In 1799, he was appointed—together with his brother, Adriaan Teyler van Hall; C. van Lennep; and J. Hooft—as a member of the First Chamber of the Representative Body (similar to the current Second Chamber [*Tweede Kamer*]). With a sigh of relief, he moved with his wife and four children to The Hague. He formally remained as the city prosecutor of Amsterdam; however, he delegated this function to G. J. Gales, Esq. In The Hague, he initially found a more quiet existence.

In the late summer of 1799, this quiet existence was horribly disturbed. It had been known for quite some time in The Hague that the English and the Russians wanted to land their armies on the Dutch coast, and it had been decided to vigorously resist that. With this purpose in mind, a small Batavian (Southern Holland) / French Army (*Bataafs / Frans Legertje*) was formed under the supreme command of the French general Brune and the Batavian generals Daendels and Dumonceau. At the end of August, the allied fleet appeared before the city of Bergen in Holland. Aboard one of the battleships was the son of Prince Willem V.

During the night of 30 August, there was a heavy pounding on the door of Maurits's house. It was a courier with a letter from Daendels. The landing was successful, and the situation was very precarious. General Brune did not dare to launch a counteroffensive, and Daendels recommended that they to move the seat of government deeper into the south (e.g., Breda).

Immediately Maurits consulted with some friends, and the courier returned that same night to Daendels with the message that he should not give an inch and that armed citizens would come to help out in a few days.

The next day, there prevailed a sense of defeat in the Inner Court (*Binnenhof*), and Maurits had difficulty suppressing his laughter when hotheaded, pro-French colleagues who never had a good word for him anxiously shook his hand and asked "Is there any news?"

Quickly he traveled with a small commission from both chambers and the minister of war from Batavia, Pyman, to the north. After arriving in Haarlem, they found a thousand armed citizens on the Grote Markt preparing for the journey north. Maurits climbed onto the terrace of the city hall there and gave a passionate speech, which was loudly applauded.[9] Immediately they continued their journey along country roads.

We'll let him tell it to you in his own words:

> *That evening of the same day the commission departed for Alkmaar and because it was dark, the cavalry leading the way followed by the carriages were lit up by torches, the reflection of which shined on the weapons and helmets of the cavalry, and in that pitch dark night along the curves of the dunes of Bakkum and Castricum created a display that to everyone, in an excitable and at the same time anxious state, made a remarkable impression.*

They had a highly disturbed General Brune awakened. The French generals did not know the tradition of citizen investigators, who, as authorized representatives, can hold inspections in our republic. They relayed the message that said that auxiliary troops were on the way and that an attack needed to be made. The First Chamber member Van Leyden van Westbarendrecht, who was the most conversant in French, spoke, and finally, Brune promised that he would do what he could "aussitôt que la prudence l'ordonnera."

Early in the morning of 4 September, the commission inspected the outposts. They were encamped outdoors. It was cold, and it rained. Luckily, food was available. Maurits saw among the volunteers Van Meurs, his erstwhile clerk and the son of a buyer of ironware in Amsterdam. The "enthusiastic youngster" died in the bloody battle of 19 September.

---

9   No matter how good the intention of the armed citizens might have been, actual fighting never occurred. They did make themselves useful in guarding the prisoners of war and transports. The Dutch essentially had no tradition on the battlefield and rather hired troops from Germany or Switzerland. It is a different case with the Royal Dutch Navy. As a seafaring nation, we have made history.

The return trip to The Hague proceeded quickly, and a report was made; Maurits, by acclamation, was elected chairman of the First Chamber.

During his stay at the headquarters of General Brune, he asked his secretary, Veru, to first notify him, by special courier, the outcome of the battle; shortly after 19 September, he learned that the counterattack was successful. Two thousand enemies were killed, and a similar number were imprisoned. The prisoners of war were very concerned about their fate:

> *Some begged for forgiveness, making the sign of the guillotine. They are very surprised that we are not barbarians. Long Live the Republic, signed Veru.*

Maurits made his way to the pulpit in the chamber and announced the good news.

During a victory party in The Hague in honor of General Brune, he made a passionate toast, in Dutch, to the Batavian general Dumonceau, the real victor, and not the wimpy and wavering General Brune.

Maurits could not stand Brune. He not only failed as a general, but it was also suspected that Brune was bought by the English to ensure a safe retreat.

Worse was the fact that General Brune was plotting with the pro-French Dutchmen to subordinate the Batavian Republic under the power of Paris. Maurits learned of these plans thanks to an English colonel living in The Hague, "Commissioner of the English Government," who had an excellent spy ring. It was a highly odd situation because, according to our notes, the colonel stayed quietly in The Hague during the landing in Bergen; armies fought, and diplomats stayed behind. The dealings with him were naturally very discrete, and sadly, there is no mention of his name in his daybook.

On a Sunday, 10 November 1799, just only two months after the battle at Bergen, Maurits dined with Krayenhoff at his country house in Rijswijk. During the dinner, the English colonel came breathlessly running in with the message that General Brune was planning a coup d'état the next day. Cavalry and other troops were advancing from the south to occupy The Hague. The colonel had a list with him with the names of those who would be imprisoned. Maurits immediately informed the executives of the regime. The guards blocked the outer and inner courts, and the commanding officer of the city, General du Ry, prepared the city's defenses. The pro-French representatives were feeling strong, and now they, without being afraid, mockingly asked again, "Citizen Van Hall, is there any news?"

A few days later, a comical denouement occurred in the chamber; he found himself as a regular member—Daendels was the president—when the ambassador of the Court of Spain, Knight d'Andraga, appeared in the gallery and dropped a card written in French down to Maurits. It said, "I have momentous information!" Maurits hastened upstairs and heard that on behalf of General Bonaparte, a Colonel Dumoulin had arrived in The Hague with the message that Bonaparte, as France's consul, had taken over the command and demanded that General Brune strictly obey orders. "Brune still wavers," added d'Andraga, "but he better reconcile himself."

Maurits rushed down to tell the news to his friends in the chamber, and the joy was clearly visible in their faces. This naturally was noted by the opponents, who now anxiously asked him, "Is there any news?" He then lightheartedly answered, "Nothing exceptional, except your coup has come to an end." The questioners turned pale. After the meeting, the events in Paris became known. Brune obeyed, and the conspiracy collapsed.

In this manner, the Batavian Republic was saved for the second time.

In The Hague, Maurits met new friends, and he delighted in telling about the elderly author Betje Wolff and Aagje Deken. The ladies previously fled to France, but when they wanted to return to their fatherland, it appeared that their capital had disappeared so totally that they could not afford the ticket home. A committee arranged for their repatriation, and upon their arrival in The Hague, Maurits made sure there was sufficient money in their home; his rich colleague Van Leyden van Westbarendrecht contributed the most.

During those days, the renowned actor Ward Bingley and his sister-in-law, the Dutch actress Wattier Ziesenis, performed regularly in The Hague. Once, Maurits brought them to the house of Betje Wolff.

> At this first meeting the author of "Sara Burgerhart" was quite taken aback that the famous actor not only was ignorant of the French language but also in the theory of his art, and was a stranger to the written works covering his art. It was charming to see how this small, of yellow color, old, but very alive Betje Wolff with her alert eyes widening in surprise, moving restlessly in her arm chair, and then with difficulty could not believe that not art but nature had formed the actor, of which no example existed in the 18th century.

Betje Wolff needed to do something about this, and she promptly translated for Wattier Ziesenis the memoirs of the French actress Clairon. As thanks, Wattier regularly sent the old ladies free tickets to the theater.

Betje Wolff called Maurits the Chosen One among the Chosen, and after her death in 1804, he received the privilege to read before the Amsterdam Division of the Department of the Batavian Company for Language and Poetry (de Amsterdamsche Afdeling van de Bataafsche Maatschappij voor Taal en Dichtkunst) his eulogy honoring Betje Wolff.

Raising his children was taking more and more of his time. He assigned his oldest son Floris for his studies to the French clergyman Merkus in Voorburg. It was always a thorn in Maurits's eye that he did not master French well, and this may be one of the reasons why, in later years, he refused the position of ambassador to Paris. The nine-year-old Floris was also a regular visitor of Betje Wolff, and although half a century in age separated them, they became the best of friends. Betje enjoyed the intellect and quick wit of Floris (the subsequent secretary of state), and she dedicated her translation of the *Kleine Bruyere* to him.

Around this time, Elizabeth, the beloved wife of Maurits, was diagnosed with cancer, and after a long illness, she died in 1802.

The many concerns made him decide to resign from his various positions, and he succeeded in a somewhat-strange way; he was, against his wishes, chosen in 1801 to be a member of the representative body for Amsterdam, though he refused to take a seat. The chamber, with an administrative order, summoned him to appear. He stayed away. A month later, he was dismissed from this post along with the post of prosecutor of Amsterdam even though his term of office had not expired; moreover, as a punishment, his right to vote was taken away. With regards to the latter, he was not overly bothered for a few months later, he took, as a citizen who was not entitled to vote, a seat in a commission organizing the management of the department.

He moved to Amsterdam and lived again in the big house on the Herengracht, between the Bergstraat and the Blauwburgwal, which was now Number 127.[10]

Maurits van Hall owed much to his older brother, Adriaan, who had became a respectable citizen of Amsterdam. He was a member of the city council, church warden of the Nieuwezijds Kapel, commissioner of the Exchange Bank (*Wissel Bank*) and the towpath to Haarlem, and a member of the provincial board. He always spoke of him with great honor until he commented that it was such a shame that his brother, Adriaan, did not do well after 1803. What went wrong? It stayed a mystery until 1951 when we got a copy of a book that was published about Engel van de Stadt, a shipowner and regent. We then understood the silence of Maurits; it was because Adriaan became involved with privateering and even piracy.

---

[10] The name of the house was Hardebollen, and it was previously occupied by the family of Jacob Bicker Raye, the author of the famous daybook of the eighteenth century. The first occupant was named Adriaan W. Hardebol. The house has a doorstep with a double staircase, and there are three windows on both sides of the front door. On both sides of the rear of the house, two small wings were built for the toilets, which one could only access through the rooms. He lived there for the rest of his life.

Adriaan Teyler van Hall and Engel van de Stadt were able to obtain in 1803 a permit from the government that authorized them to capture English commercial vessels. They focused especially on the busy trade between England and the Scandinavian countries. They equipped two ships, *De Unie* and *De Wraak*, and gave the command to a Frenchman, Jean Saint Faust, who was a fearless and hard sailor. Business went so well that shortly thereafter, they set up the Batavian Privateering Shipping Company (*Bataafse Kaaprederij*) with a capital of forty thousand guilders and expanded their fleet to eight vessels.

We recite the following passages from the aforementioned book:

> On 19 September, 1803 Saint Faust departed with his ships the "Vlie." Almost immediately he had to fight a heavily fortified English Cutter with a crew of 80 to a 100, to the east of the island Terschelling. When he had a chance to board, a downpour occurred, which the English used to escape. Regrettably there were a few wounded and the shelling caused damage. On 20 September Saint Faust captured "The Sally of Portland," which flew the American flag, but did not have adequate ship's papers. It had a cargo worth fl. 200,000. On 24 September Saint Faust ended up in an English convoy. He was able to escape the English Escort that was hunting him down. On 25 September Saint Faust captured the English cargo ship "Good Intent." This ship was underway from Sweden to Scotland carrying iron, potash, and wood. Saint Faust brought this prize to Kristiansand. Engel van de Stadt sold this ship on 27 October, 1803 for fl. 8,000 to Captain Johan Block of Jengum in East Friesland. On 1 October the "British Star" was captured and on 4 October the "William and Thomas." In addition, the privateer had chased five English ships onto the beach . . . .

> . . . . He also did not hesitate, when the opportunity arose, to attack an English battle ship and that was especially the case on 3 March, 1804, when Saint Faust with his division along the Norwegian coast attacked the English frigate "Amethes" under the command of Captain Campbell carrying 20 canons for 32, 28 and 18 pound cannonballs and caused it to flee, even though the frigate was far more powerful than the combined fleet of Saint Faust. These were the "Bataafse Trouw" with 12 canons for 12 and 2 pound cannonballs, the "Unie" with 16

canons, the "Deugd" with 4 canons for 8 pound cannonballs, and the "Eer" with 8 canons for 2 pound cannonballs. Close to three hours the battle continued with the frigate firing 1144 and the combined privateers 380 pounds. When the firing of the Brit stopped and called for a retreat, Saint Faust gave the sign to pursue the vessel and overpower it, but it turned out that the damage to the masts and rigging was too great and the frigate was able to escape. It had 25 fatalities and 60 to 70 injured sailors; the losses of the privateers were barely mentioned . . . .

The setbacks of the shipping company consisted not only from the loss of their vessels. The captured prizes were not always safe from the enemy. In August/September 1804 the privateer vessel "De Eer" had captured the English vessel "The British Star." The victorious crew had brought the vessel over the dry banks off the coast of Harlingen. On 13 September, 1804, the English pulled an audacious stunt by sending 40 men in a fishing boat to the captured vessel and over powered the small crew. At first they tried to get the boat over the dry banks and when that did not succeed they set it on fire. The Directors who still had a prize in Delfzijl for anchor the "Peggy and Polly" and their privateer "De Eer" considered their situation precarious. Dutch fishermen and their fishing boats and the population along the coast were often employed by the English and one encountered in many manners sabotage.

Complaints were received about the harshness of the head of the fleet, Saint Faust, and also about the fact that he captured Danish and German commercial vessels. He showed a prime example of pure piracy when he stopped three Dutch coastal vessels who at last had reached the safe waters of Holland. The cargo in these ships was meant for merchants in Amsterdam, and in response to their indignant protests, they received this laconic answer—if they offered something worthwhile, they could have their ships and cargo back!

Adriaan van Hall and Engel van der Stadt had gone too far and obviously could not control Saint Faust. The government expelled Saint Faust, and the shipping company was dissolved.

Saint Faust ended up imprisoned by the English. When he, in the prison of Chatham in 1807, requested a bill of exchange for sixty-five pound sterling from Adriaan van Hall and Engel van der Stadt, they refused to pay. Ingratitude is the wage of the world!

After the crowning of Lodewijk Napoleon, Adriaan van Hall established a new shipping company, Crusade and Privateering (*Kruistocht en Kaapvaart*), with a capital of fifty thousand guilders. He did not have much success because the English had had enough of him and wiped his fleet off the ocean.

When it became known that the top official R. J. Schimmelpenninck was going to be replaced by King Lodewijk, Maurits had a fierce protest printed and distributed it widely. It stayed with a protest and, through a weird misunderstanding, Maurits was actually the first one to greet the new King at his official welcoming into Amsterdam. He was accompanied by N. Sanderman, Esq., and H. Ravekes; they were the chief executives of the Society for the Benefit of the Common Good (*Mij. Tot Nut van 't Algemeen*). To the annoyance of the other authorities present, King Lodewijk thought they were the most important functionaries, and the two were not successful in explaining what exactly the Mij. Tot Nut van 't Algemeen was. "Where is this society situated?" asked the King, upon which Ravekes answered, "Par toute la République, Majesté!" The King started to laugh; the Dutchmen were obviously not yet used to the monarchy.

Despite his protests, Maurits became a good friend of Lodewijk. He actually felt sorry for the man, who did not aspire to the assignment forced upon him and could not manage it well.

Some years previously, Maurits was appointed count of the sea dike and president director of the big sea lock in Muiden (*dijkgraaf van den Zeedijk en president-directeur der groote zeesluis te Muiden*), and in this function, he had to receive Lodewijk there. On the order of Napoleon, forts were currently being built, and when Lodewijk halted at one of the fortifications, tenants rushed forward. They began swearing at the King in the most rough way and holding on to the door of the carriage so that he could not get out, and a lady concluded the meeting with the words, "You better make sure I get money for the land that I have been working." Dismayed, the King asked his aide-de-camp, Bloys van Treslong, who sat next to him, "Qu'est ce qu'elle dit?" upon which he said that the lady, in the most respectful manner, asked if it would suit his majesty to explore ways to ameliorate her fiscal difficulties with the loss of her land. A diplomat, this Bloys!

Maurits and General Krayenhoff cautiously came closer and heard Lodewijk say, "General, tomorrow a report!"

Within three days, she had her money.

The reason for the visit of Lodewijk to Muiden was the hurricane of 1808, which caused substantial devastation.

During the night of this flood disaster, a farmer mayor (*boeren-maire*) sent a complaint to the judge in charge of the Amstelland (*landdrost van Amstelland*) that the Count of the Dikes (*dijkgraaf*) was not present. The judge immediately dispatched Baron Van Pallandt van Keppel to the flooded area, who could see neither the Count of the Dikes nor the directors overseeing the polders (*Heemraad*). On one of the endangered places, he addressed a man dressed as if in mourning and who, while tied to another man, was busy working. "Where is the Dijkgraaf?" he asked. "He stands in front of you" was the answer.

In 1810, Maurits receives a letter from R. J. Schimmelpenninck from Paris; it reported that the annexation by France was around the corner, and again he published another protest.

King Lodewijk departed and left with Maurits the papers regarding his abdication. In 1814, after the liberation, he received permission from King Willem I to send them to the ex-King Lodewijk, who was residing in Rome.

The annexation by France was unacceptable to Maurits, and he refused to cooperate. In the coming three years, he established closer ties with the ever-growing party that strived for the return of Orange (*Oranje*); as a lawyer, he defended Orange clients when they came into conflict with the occupier. During the French occupation, he did not want to accept any public office. This is a position that we understand quite well. Still we ask ourselves, didn't those who did accept offices serve the Fatherland better—in addition to running more risk?

In Middelburg, for example, J. H. Schorer, Esq., accepted the position of mayor. He found himself in a difficult position when in 1810, after the unsuccessful landing of the English on the island of Walcheren, Napoleon came to teach him, in the most uncouth manner, a lesson on the bad attitude of the population, including Schorer. Schorer asserted himself so angrily and furiously that Napoleon apologized the next day for his rude tone—something that Napoleon not often did, if ever.

In 1814, Schorer became the first Governor of the King in the Province of Zeeland and President of the Knighthood.

The NSBers—members of the National-Socialistic Movement, followers of Hitler and the Nazis—often wanted to compare themselves with the patriots and the Batavians. This comparison does not fly. The revolutionary ideas of freedom and equality that were born in France lived in our people. In 1801, the Prince of Orange recognized the new mandate, which helped with the acceptance of the patriots, and Orange became the symbol of liberation and unity in the battle against the dictator Napoleon.

The national-socialists did not have many members in our country and were detested by the rest. Queen Wilhelmina held the torch of our best cultural and historical traditions high, and she, supported by all of us, fought the battle to the bitter end against Hitler and his NSB followers.

The successor to King Lodewijk was Prince le Brun, who became the Regent and Chief Chancellor. He and Maurits soon became friends. He called him the Good Graybeard and he often invited him to eat, which (and this part was said with some bitterness) was scantily provided for and soon finished. There was, after all, a blockade established by the English.

The relationship with Prince le Brun came of good use when he had to defend his clients.

In 1811, it so happened that a young shipowner in Muiden, by the name of Selleger, came to him for advice about his ship that had been confiscated and have Maurits release it. Maurits was not suspicious until he suddenly was ordered to appear at the headquarters of General Durutte, the military governor, which was located on the Herengracht, opposite the Plantage. With the most rude threats, the General commanded to give him the name of the shipowner because—and this fact came to light later—the shipowner had a thriving smuggling operation with England and carried also many Dutch West Indies colonists home. Maurits refused and said, "Les lois de l'Empire ne permettent pas à un avocat de révéler les secrets lui confiés [*The laws of the empire do not allow a lawyer to reveal the secrets of his client*]."

Not assured with the result of the meeting, he rushed over to Prince le Brun, who invited him and General Durutte for a meal and sat him next to the grim general. Not a word was ever mentioned about the incident.

A perilous story was about the arrest of Johan Valckenaer, Esq., the former representative of the Batavian Republic to the Spanish court, following a revolt of the Orange-minded people in the neighborhood of Alphen. He was transferred to the state prison (*verbeterhuis*) under the accusation that he was the head and participant of the revolt—an accusation that carried the death penalty.

After a battle of words with the director of the police, Devilliers Duterrage, Maurits announced that there was a horrible misunderstanding: Valckenaer was so vehemently anti-Orange that with a change of government that would put Orange in charge, Valckenaer would have been the first to be strung up a tree; to wit, he had, together with Prof. Voorda, published a legal opinion that stated that Prince Willem V deserved a death sentence. This made a deep impression on the police, and that evening, the perhaps-not-so-innocent Valckenaer was released.

We read that Mr. Devilliers Duterrage had an honorable and humane character that was not in agreement with his assigned, hateful position, and he especially did not share the conduct of the cruel and hated de Celles. On 16 October 1813, he, with the aid of Maurits, was allowed to leave the country unhindered.

In those days, it was a rough period. On the Damrak stood a herring cart with the first herring of the season (*Hollandse Nieuwe*). When the herring man cut off the head of one with a hefty slash, he yelled to the delight of the bystanders, "I wish this was the head of Napoleon." An informer reported this to the French police, upon which he was arrested and sentenced.

Prince le Brun could not prevent Maurits's grief that his son Floris, as a so-called Garde d'Honneur, had to leave the country. Maurits moved heaven and earth to prevent this. He had already paid three thousand guilders for a replacement, and because of other smart reasons, he figured he would receive an exemption. He was not successful. One did not trust him and explained that if he undertook something against the French regime, his son would pay the penalty. These circumstances influenced him not to participate in the resistance to the French occupation. He mentioned this in his answer to Falck, when he received an urgent appeal for help.

Thus Floris, together with his neighboring friend Claude Crommelin, was forced to be conscripted in the Garde d'Honneur. He did not want to go underground because his father, with his large family, would end up in trouble. His father accompanied him and Claude to Beusichem, which resulted in a dramatic farewell: *"He is very fearsome that he will never see him again."* Floris beseeched his father not to be overcome with this hostage taking. He said he would take care of himself. He did exactly that: he escaped and made sure he was well-off. Once back in Holland, his father promptly paid all the bills.

It is interesting to learn a little about the adventures of young Floris. After the upheaval in Holland started, the Gardes d'Honneur were disarmed and transported as prisoners to the south. In Bourges, he was able to escape and ventured to the east while dressed in a stately black dress coat with a red ribbon. At one time, the gendarmes caught his trail, but a kindhearted lady innkeeper hid him in a deep closet in between her voluminous robes. He hid there with his spaniel, who always accompanied him, and the animal, which was very watchful, was dead quiet, so they were not discovered. Walking was too slow for him, and then he encountered near Macon a French country nobleman, seated on a handsome horse. His presence inspired confidence in Floris and decided to ask for help, especially since he was almost out of money. The Frenchman agreed to sell him his horse based on Floris's good countenance, but due to the risk, he said some more money than the actual worth would have to be remitted from Holland. With this horse, he escaped to Lausanne, where the trading house

Goll & Cie provided him with money and shelter. The son of Mr. Goll was also a Garde d'Honneur and a friend of Floris.

In 1813, the liberation occurred. It became clamorous in the city. The little customs offices were burned down. Maurits went immediately to the Palace on the Dam and offered the viceroy of Napoleon, Prince le Brun, a safe conduct to France. (In Vianen, after all, he learned how to write safe-conduct passes!) This could be done secretly and in disguise or openly to which risks are naturally associated with. He recommended the former and prepared a carriage with four horses that was to be accompanied by four mounted soldiers. Early in the morning of the day of the Prince's departure, he positioned himself with his son Adriaan and some armed friends at the rear entrance of the palace. The carriage arrived. The old and sick le Brun boarded it, but once seated, he pushed the curtain aside to—after his old custom—wave benignly to the public. He was recognized, and the tension mounted till a woman of the people yelled, "Just let the bum go. He has not hurt us."

Before his departure, Prince le Brun had to solemnly swear that he would immediately do his utmost to make sure that Floris and the other hostages would be sent unscathed home upon his arrival in Paris. Floris did not wait for this. He organized his own repatriation from his hideout in Switzerland.

When King Willem I arrived in Amsterdam, Maurits Cornelis was summoned to the palace. The King raised the situation surrounding the English-Russian landing. Maurits was momentarily demure because he knew that the King had been fully informed about his role by Mr. Van Heeckeren van Walien, yet Maurits said, "*If the venture had succeeded, Your Majesty would be now a Regent without power, and not a Sovereign Monarch.*" This statement produced a smile and, as such, was well received.

Shortly thereafter, he was invited to a dinner in the Palace in Amsterdam. The other guests were Professor D. J. van Lennep, Esq.; J. Bondt, Esq.; J. Walraven; and Mr. Johan Valckenaer. Princess Wilhelmina, widow of Prince Willem V, actually had some objections against the latter because she had a hard time forgetting his stand in 1795 even though he somewhat made up for it in the uprising in Alphen. Likewise, our Maurits initially approached her hesitantly. "*But this noble, wise and civil Lady, took the lead and said amicably: 'What a change in such a few years,' and praised Amsterdam and the spirit of the citizens.*"

While she was sitting on the sofa and conversing with Maurits, the young Prince of Orange, dressed in the uniform of the hussars, approached; with grandmotherly pride, she recited Wellington's laudatory words about the bravery of her grandson—and deservedly so.

Today there are still descendants of patriots who, in their affection for the House of Orange, are ashamed of their ancestors. May they be comforted by the comments of King Willem I and Princess Wilhelmina.

The reader most likely will have guessed it: Maurits obtained the trust and friendship of King Willem I and, as we read on, later also of Willem II and Willem III. Was he a Talleyrand? A slavish submissiveness did not suit him; he always spoke his mind straightforwardly. This became instantly apparent after the liberation of 1813, when Fannius Scholten, Esq., and J. M. Kemper were deputized by The Hague to go to Amsterdam with the message that said that only the Orange flag could fly. On behalf of a number of citizens, Maurits protested, and the time-honored state flag flew next to it. *The Fatherland has been restored by Orange, but it cannot become a total Orange-upheaval.* Apart from that, the evening became a very joyful victory dinner with the gentlemen from The Hague. Jan Bondt, Esq., brought fine Varina cigars along, of which he had stocked up a big supply before the French imposed tobacco regulations, and he sheltered them with a number of lady friends. Soon one could cut through the smoke, to the discomfort of Falck; luckily for him, Mrs. Kemper came along, and the gentlemen had to extinguish their cigars. The dinner took place in a hotel on the Doelenstraat, where Magistrate de Celles had his headquarters (just like SS General Rauter in the Second World War), and it was to chase away the bad odor of that man that there was such heavy smoking.

Although Maurits did not want to accept public positions, he carried out many assignments for King Willem I in financial and legal areas—not only in government matters but also in the private affairs of King Willem I.

He had already occupied himself with many financial transactions, and once this almost cost him his life. To wit, he represented in 1813 the holders of Swedish bonds that were not being repaid properly. On a certain afternoon, around three o'clock, he was in the study of his house, De Hardebollen, on the Herengracht. Only two of his young children and an old deaf maid were in the house when the latter announced that a male person wanted to talk to him. Not suspecting anything bad, he let him come in, whereupon the man jumped at Maurits with a big knife. Maurits immediately grabbed the chair on which he sat and landed it with a thunderous blow on the head of the villain. He fell to the ground; Maurits could only barely restrain him by placing a knee on his chest and strangling him with his scarf. The deaf maid could not hear his cries for help, and a long half hour later, his son Adriaan, returning from the stock exchange, arrived and helped him. Together they had the biggest trouble keeping the brute succumbed, and only at four o'clock did the police, warned earlier, make an appearance. The man had been ruined with the purchase of the Swedish funds and wanted to take his revenge out on Maurits. At the request of Maurits, he was not prosecuted.

In 1815, Napoleon escaped from Elba and advanced to the north with an army. The government securities' values declined considerably, so a number of bankruptcies were imminent; the government had a difficult time receiving financing for the warfare.

Maurits approached his friend Jan Bondt, Esq., (whose daughter meanwhile had married his son Floris) with a plan to upgrade the stock-exchange rates of the sovereign funds.

Together they went to the King, who, out of his private capital, made five hundred thousand guilders available. With this amount, an appointed committee manipulated the stock exchange and achieved the desired result. After the Battle of Waterloo, the King got back his half million guilders. In that year, Maurits was appointed knight in the Order of the Dutch Lion (*ridder in de Orde van de Nederlandse Leeuw*).

Maurits was now at home a lot and spent much time taking care of the upbringing of his children. He had satisfying materials to work with. Five sons were studying at the University of Amsterdam under the special tutelage of Professor D. J. van Lennep, Esq. On 9 November 1844, Professor Van Lennep celebrated his fiftieth anniversary as a professor, during which time he was the soul and driving force of the university. We can read this in a paean that Maurits wrote, and here are two verses of it:

> *I see an oak, still with leaves*
> *Approaching the top of old age*
> *And still with the splendor of the majestic wood.*
> *How! His fifty three years,*
> *Just like a mirage, navigated through all.*
> *And I, from the CRAS and BURMAN'S school,*
> *Was allowed to lead you into the Court Room,*
> *In Amstel's Marbel Capitol.*

It continues like this for many verses; he commemorated the country place of Van Lennep, Manpad, and especially the wise lessons given to his sons.

Soon a number of his sons stepped up to the forefront just like their father. We mention here Floris, the later secretary of state, and Jacob, JD, PhD. The latter was already appointed, at the age of twenty-four, to the post of professor of Roman languages and current law, first in Amsterdam and then in Utrecht, where he remained until his death. And furthermore, Herman became a professor of botany and estate management in Groningen. On Anne Maurits, we will devote a separate chapter.

In 1831, Maurits became President of the Court of Justice in Amsterdam and also the Minister of the State. He was now fulfilling the role of gray eminence, and he most likely would have ended his life with this role if not for the fact that in 1842, his son Floris was appointed Secretary of State for Justice.

Time and again King Willem I had asked him to become a member of the chamber, but he refused each time. Now he asked King Willem II for a seat in the First Chamber, and by royal decree, he was appointed a seat. As a lion, he defended new bills presented by his son Floris, and this became particularly important when in 1844, Floris Adriaan was appointed Secretary of State for Finances.

He stayed on till 1848 and became, just as his son Floris, a member of a commission that would review the revising of the Constitution.

Perhaps the great sorrow over the persecution of his son Anne Maurits Cornelis and his early death influenced him to become involved, even at his advanced age, in changing the Constitution, which did not have guarantees for freedom of religion; there will be more about this later.

He stayed often again in The Hague and supported Floris wherever he could, also in the relationship with the Royal House.

In the following, we mention three paragraphs out of his daybook.

On 13 October 1842, he was invited to the palace in The Hague to say good-bye to Princess Sophie of Orange, who had gotten married to the heir grand duke (erf-*groothertog*) of Saxen-Weimar-Eisenach; on the fifteenth, she departed with her spouse to Weimar.

After the meal, this lovely lady "with tears flowing, bade everyone affectionately farewell, Maurits with a handshake thanking him, as she said, for the 'sweet words' he spoke to her."

Our elderly Maurits was obviously a charmer.

During these years, he had to say farewell more than once.

On 15 June of the same year, he was invited by King Willem I, who resigned in 1840, to the Royal Palace Het Loo to once again talk about the old times. After a simple meal, at which the servants were not dressed in livery and which lasted till six o'clock, the King wittily spoke of events that happened in the past. At the parting, the King took Maurits's hand in a solid grip and didn't let go. Both men had tears in their eyes. And for those who do not want to believe this,

Maurits reported that Knight van Rappard and A. W. Baron van Pallandt van Beerse, among others, witnessed them.

On 15 May 1845, he paid a visit to his son Floris Adriaan, who lived in Kruidenberg, near Santpoort (later the estate came into the possession of the Cremer family, who built a new house named Duin en Kruidberg). Actually, it was a three-way celebration. It was Floris Adriaan's birthday, it was his and his wife's thirty-year marriage anniversary, and it was a farewell party for Mr. J. J. Rochussen, who as the Governor General would be departing for "Indië," now Indonesia.

A shadow, however, fell over the day because Jan Bondt, Esq., the father-in-law of Floris Adriaan, had a very difficult time traveling to Santpoort due to his bad health; a short time later, he passed away. The health of Alida van Hall was just as bad. When she returned to The Hague, King Willem II was so startled by her appearance that he offered her Zorgvliet, formerly built by Cats and situated in the Scheveningen dunes, so she could escape the tumultuous The Hague and recuperate. It was no use; within a few weeks, she also died.

After the revision of the Constitution, the eighty-year-old Maurits withdrew from politics. King Willem II appointed him Commandant in the Order of the Dutch Lion (*commandeur in de Orde van de Nederlandse Leeuw*). With renewed energy, he started writing again.

He had written unbelievably much in his life; over a hundred books and publications appeared by his hand. For each occasion, he created a poem. To our taste, his style is too pompous; his sentence construction, too convoluted. Therefore, it is difficult to read. He found his inspiration as a poet in the book of Psalms in 1771, which he knew by heart. Undoubtedly, he was influenced by the great Bilderdijk, though he regretted his acerbity. He admonished him as follows in a poem:

> *And thou, o Grey Beard, who we name with reverence.*
> *Ah, why does your eminent poetry sound so acrid?*
> *Force us, again, your poetry to roam royally:*
> *And follow the queen of flowers;*
> *She of good scent and radiance, but disregard her thorns!*

Maurits was, at that time, impassioned by the flourishing practice of the classics. People were tired of the somewhat-vague and spineless mimicry of the French literature of the seventeenth and eighteenth centuries and sought more concise and muscular poems.

In the French period, he was a member of the literary society Concordia et Liberrate together with, among others, Van Lennep, Loots, Falck, Elout, and F. van der Poll. The building was in the St. Luciensteeg. The society was dissolved in 1812 due to the fear of the French. For years he was a member of the Society of Dutch Literature (*Maatschappij der Nederlandsche Letterkunde*), the Royal Dutch Institute (*Koninklijk Nederlandsch Instituut*), and the Dutch Society of the Sciences (*Hollandsche Maatschappij van Wetenschappen*).

H. J. Koenen was of the opinion that Maurits, thanks to some of his poems (and, among others, the celebration song he composed to mark the two hundred and fifty years of existence of the university of Leiden [*feestzang ter gelegenheid van het tweehonderdvijftigjarige bestaan van de Leidsche Hoogeschool*], "de Aloe en W. Bilderdijk, Esq.," and "Gedicht aan Koning Willem I"), occupied the first place on the Zangberg in those days. We take this with a grain of salt because the laudatory speech (*lofrede*) was a lot of puff; people did not like criticism. This frame of mind became disastrous for Maurits during a duel of the pens that he conducted with Groen van Prinsterer. He had namely written a book about "Hendrick, Count van Brederode Co-Founder of the Netherlands Freedom" in which he defended the premise that the history writers had belittled and maligned the deeds of the Van Brederodes and glorified the role of the Oranges.

With the permission of the King, Groen published a number of letters from the King's personal archive that threw a whole different light on Brederode and negated Maurits's position. They formed the basis of the thoroughly documented reply of Groen to Van Hall.

Maurits was angry, and he rebuked Groen, saying that these letters never should have been made public. They were, after all, private correspondence, and it was inappropriate, unlawful, and contrary to justice and common practice to do this. He was of the opinion that these letters should not be part of the proceedings. But then the so-dangerous broadsword of Groen van Prinsterer glimmered in the face of its opponent, on top of which he was the family friend of the Van Halls in the Hardebollen on the Herengracht:

> *Why do you force me, o, honorable greybeard of seventy six years, to contradict you and to tear down your work. The historian must speak truthfully, the whole truth. That is a demand of the science and the right of the descendants.*

The eulogist lost against the historian. For Maurits, this was a bitter pill, especially since all the articles were published and republished. This polemic took place in 1844 and did not, as evidenced in earlier writing, have a negative effect in his relationship with the members of the Royal Palace.

When Maurits did not write for the public, his pompous style disappeared. We cite the following little poem that he sent to his daughter Margaretha Jongeneel-van Hall because her daughter Chrisje was so scared when she saw his lithograph. And indeed, he had a stern and aristocratic bearing, which was so appropriate for the President of the Courts and a Statesman.

> *But, Margarethe! If the dear child*
> > *In her innocence*
> *Sees in black ink, my image*
> > *And therefore cries startled*
> *Then you say with a calm look*
> > *"Rest assured, Chrisje*
> *That mouth, that appears so dark*
> > *Has kissed you whole heartedly"*
> > *Etc.*

His rhymes appeals to us more than his poems.

What transpired during a literary meeting (which he attended frequently)? The daybook of the student Nicolaas Beets gives us the following report:

7 January, 1836

Monday, 4 January, I arrived. I was deathly sick with a cold, which was not noticeable in my voice, but we have to take it as it falls and the Amsterdam public needs to be pleased. The Society of Beautiful Arts holds her public meetings in the Building of the Society for the Common Good [Gebouw der Maatschappij tot Nut van't Algemeen]. *Though I have to say, they do not blaspheme the plebian pronouncements of the Common Do-Gooders—"Nutters"— but bring their own furniture (actually I believe from the Free Masons), a beautiful mahogany showpiece, in which the orator or poet is pyramided between two lying down sphinxes, each holding in their graceful claws a candle holder for three candles, while, so that he would not lack light, a gas lantern hangs above his head. The Society has become since Abraham des Amorie van der Hoeven very fashionable with the prominent citizens* [beau monde] *and we had an audience of three to four hundred people, of which 200 were ladies. It was something else than in Alphen. Thou should have seen our procession, when we entered the hall at seven fifteen. First the Dutch great prolific writer, the charming Van Kampen; thereafter the prolific poet, the exceptional Van der Hoop—oh my Heavens! Then I followed, definitely at that moment the Dutch poet with the worst cold of all poets. Subsequently the Secretary of the Society, Van Hasselt, Esq. Then the stately tall figure of the grey Knight Maurits Cornelis van Hall, Esq., and finally closing the procession Mr. Fabius, also an Esq and also a Knight and also grey and also tall. Van Kampen held a short New Years Wish, and after that Van der Hoop climbed onto the beautiful mahogany chair. He read the first verse of a new story in rhyme, in the manner of his "Slot van Yselmonde" titled: The Danish Vesper, from long ago. All the persons who appeared in the song were terribly strong, had bloodcurdling swords on their sides, and to me were real savage warriors. What struck me was that the poet used images from the animal world. There were deer, tigers, lions and lionesses, bears, dogs, eagles, pigeons, singing birds, vultures, wild boars, hares, rabbits and all sorts of rabble; add two sphinxes, about which I reported to you, and you will comprehend that there were many animals on the lectern. Van der Hoop reads airily and unclear. He does not use gestures well and often ridiculously so.*

We stately leave the podium and proceed to the chambers of the management, or as we say in Alphen: "the table of the Board of Directors." We were served a pleasant glass of wine. At the stroke of nine the activities resumed, and the procession now expanded with Dr. Haakman and Mr. Van Oosterwijk Bruyn moving toward the lectern. I ascended to the place of honor, and my well known shamelessness, looking out at such a large meeting, served me well. Speaking did not cause too much difficulty as I had thought, although once in a while I produced a spurious sound. My introduction already received a good applause and also with various passages of the Poem (the translation of Parisina). The silence was heavenly. After the conclusion I talked briefly with Withuys, who appeared to want to compliment me and he presented Messrs. Jeronimo de Vries and Brester to me. After that there was an oyster feast with the Board of Directors. The old Van Hall had escaped, but Van Kampen, Van Hasselt, Fabius, Haakman and Bruyn sat with me. But the company was again expanded with des Amorie, fellow member of the Board, who had to preside over a meeting of the Missionary Society and with Heye, as a guest, who was specially invited for me. It was a very jolly party and when at one thirty the rest of the party went home, Van Hasselt, Van der Hoop, Heye and I stayed and enjoyed a couple of bottles of champagne. It was a total loquacious feast. We parted at three thirty!

The hurricane of 1808. A watercolor made by an eyewitness on the locks of the
IJ; the equivalent of todays press photo.
Collectie Atlas van Stolk

Maurits Cornelis van Hall, Esq., Heer van Heicop en Boeicop, 1768 – 1858, 50 years old from a painting by Pieneman.

Floris Adriaan van Hall, Heer van Heicop en Boeicop. Born in 1736 in Leiden, died in Amsterdam in 1808. The little poem was written by his son Maurits.

I can still approach your silhouette cheerfully, you most pious of Fathers!
With grateful tears on my face:
All what I became and stayed;
Even more than that – my innerlife,
I owe, next to God, to you.

With longer pauses and a somewhat-shaky hand, Maurits continued to write in his daybook, and the thoughts often went to the past. A certain vanity was no stranger to him, and he considered it an appropriate sentiment of his self worth.

In June 1852, he had been Count of the Dikes of Muiden for forty-eight years. His comembers of the Board of the Dikes and the directors bestowed on him a beautiful silver goblet—perhaps in the hope that he at last would resign. He did not, and his obstinacy was rewarded in 1854 when all of Muiden was decorated with flags and he received the Knights Cross with a star in the Order of the Oak Crown (*ridderkruis met de ster in de Orde van de Eikenkroon*) on behalf of King Willem III to commemorate his fifty years as Count of the Dikes.

In 1856, he made a note "with understandable pride as a father" that stated that his son Floris had been knighted.

On 19 January 1858, when he was almost ninety years old, he closed his eyes.

We nevertheless won't bid him adieu at this time because we will meet him again in the chapter on his son Anne Maurits Cornelis and in the chapter on his grandson Maurits Cornelis.

ANNE MAURITS CORNELIS VAN HALL, ESQ., 1808–1838

THE LAWYER FOR THE REFORMED AND HIS WIFE SUZE

Anne Maurits was born on 26 February, 1808 and was baptized in Zuiderkerk on 30 March.

He had an exceptionally happy and carefree youth. He was the ninth child, and after him, another seven would appear, though the large house on the canal could easily handle them all. The family spent their summer vacations either at Monikkenhof in Vianen or at Huis te Heicop.

At the age of sixteen, he was registered as a literature student in the Athenaeum Illustre in Amsterdam. After a couple of years, he changed to the study of law in Leiden with. He also registered as a student in Leiden and divided his time between Leiden and Amsterdam according to the lectures he wanted to take; in particular, he spent more time in Amsterdam with Prof. Jacob van Hall, his brother, and Prof. Den Tex. His best friends were J. W. Gefken, J. Tideman, Jan Bousquet, and B. ter Haar. He also had contact with Isaac da Costa, who was ten years older than him, and Groen van Prinsterer.

He led a joyful student life and participated in everything. He expressed his "joie de vivre" in "Ne Praeter Modum," a song of the Amsterdam Student Corps.

> Well behaved, to be a student,
> Is the true feeling of life!!!
> It is with girls and with wine
> To be a good student!!!

When was a girl indifferent
To the honorable name of a student?
Her lovely little heart is not easily persuaded
By his sweet talk in the end.

Who counts all those glances
Accompanied by a laugh and some flirting
The sweet charming glances
That is bestowed on student life.

Under the happy cheers
He valiantly fills his glass
And speaks emotionally during the cheers
The joyous language of friends.

And the sounds reverberate
With glory to the Fatherland and the King
For studying and the beautiful
He sings full heartedly.

This beautiful verse is sung along the music of "C'est l'amour"!

The year 1830 was full of events. First of all was his promotion to doctor of law with J. W. Gefken and J. de Bosch Kemper as his paranymphs. Then two happy weddings took place in De Hardebollen on the Herengracht. Sister Anna married Andreas Ch. van Braam Houckgeest, a naval officer and a holder of the Military Willems Order and, later, the State Council. Sister Johanna married the young minister Dr. J. Tideman, who was later a professor at the Remonstrants Seminarium in Amsterdam.

In the fall, when the revolution in Belgium was about to explode, Anne Maurits signed up as a volunteer in the army together with J. W. Gefken and Jan Bousquet and departed to the south.

On 31 October 1830, they arrived in good order in two steamboats in 's-Hertogenbosch. First they were quartered with citizens, but after a couple of days, they moved to the bishop's palace, "a first rate establishment."

Our volunteers never ventured further than 's-Hertogenbosch. Their assignment was limited to garrison services. Initially, Anne Maurits frequently visited prominent families in North Brabant; gradually, the friends spent more time seriously discussing religious subjects in which also Lieutenant Dudok Bousquet, a brother of Jan, and a passionate Da Costian joined in.

In this environment, Anne Maurits experienced a spiritual awakening and became aware of his inner life, and this experience guided him throughout his life. Various circumstances contributed to this. One could hear the thundering cannons in the south; several of his brothers joined the war, and his brother-in-law Van Braam Houckgeest served on a battleship on the Schelde. For the first time in his life, he was confronted with violent death. The atmosphere of the bishop's palace also encouraged the young men to consider the more serious questions of life.

The Van Halls were, from the outset, Protestants and devoted churchgoers. Admittedly, his father, the old Maurits Cornelis, was, in his youth, a follower of the then-prevalent views of freedom and enlightenment, and just like Prof. D. J. van Lennep, he was an admirer of the philosophy of the classics. He could not reconcile himself with the philosophy of Kant, which he thought could not replace, totally or in part, religion. The old Maurits, with his contemporaries, had a broader view of religion. Anne Maurits would try to bring back religion to the people.

Back in Amsterdam, he arrived at the law offices of his father and his brother Floris Adriaan. The law office was in the handsome house Saxenburg, which is now Keizersgracht 224; it was the house of Floris. Anne Maurits, who was twenty-three years old, found himself in a busy practice, with two smart teachers, and with the prospect of a successful career.

A second experience would make a major impression on his inner life: the awful cholera epidemic of 1832. While the well-off citizens of Amsterdam fled the infected city, Anne Maurits took on the care of the cholera victims in the densely populated District I (*Wijk I*) and saw up close the wretchedness of the disease. On 21 November 1832, he wrote a letter to his oldest brother, Floris Adriaan, who at that time was a captain of the armed home guard:

> *Most likely very hard times are coming and so the calamity* [He is referring to the cholera] *only serves for us to come closer to God and expect all the good from our Father in Christ, and like our forefathers supported by the bible, the outcome will be just. You know, my valued brother, that I am accused of having fanatical feelings. But I presume that you do not consider me a hypocrite. If I look around me, and I review the events of the day, than I see my so-called fanatical feelings more and more justified. Revolts and violence spreading throughout Europe; the most horrible civil wars in France and England, and a part of Germany ready to erupt, prove to me that the people, notwithstanding the so-called highly acclaimed civilization, enlightenment etc., by nature are sinners, which are the fruits of not believing in God.*

Couldn't these words have been written like this today? "Plus ca change, rien ne change!" Culture and scientific advances cannot replace religion and love of one's fellow man.

Cholera raged also in Utrecht. Among the victims were the father and sister of the seventeen-year-old Suze van Schermbeek, with whom Anne Maurits was engaged. It was a miracle that she stayed healthy. In the battle against the disease, they followed the Utrecht system, which is to say that they thought that during the illness cycle when the body gets colder and colder, only the warmth of a human body could alter the course of the disease for the better. Suze shared a bedroom with her sick sister. Amsterdam, on the other hand, implemented very strict isolation, which led to heartrending scenes when children infected with cholera were taken away from their parents so they could be cared for with warm water bottles elsewhere. We heard of one family where eleven of its twelve children successively died.

This situation made a deep impression on Anne Maurits and Suze van Schermbeek. The beautiful silver cholera medal he received from the City of Amsterdam brought little consolation.

By the end of the cholera epidemic, Anne Maurits felt a growing need to implement his new religious conversion and start the battle against the unbelievers. With these thoughts in mind, Maurits visited H. J. Koenen, and as luck would have it, he had just received a letter from Groen van Prinsterer in which the wish to create a magazine with a religious theme was expressed.

The friends put their heads together, and in May 1834, the first issue of *Dutch Voices on Religion, State, History and Literature* (*Nederlandsche Stemmen voor Godsdienst, Staat-, Geschied-, en Letterkunde*) was published under the editorships of Anne Maurits, Koenen, and Da Costa. Willem de Clercq joined the three sometime later; Ms. M. E. Kluit, his granddaughter, was the secretary of the society Reveil-Archief, and in her book *Het Reveil in Nederland,* she elaborately described all the events.

Besides subjects such as "The Creation," "The Prayer of the Lord," "The Scripture, the Spirit and the Church," and "The Day of Judgement," we also find covered "The Government and the Law," "The Profession of Judges," and "The Poems of Bilderdijk." The pieces are not signed, so we cannot figure out which ones were written by Van Hall. The editors had agreed to this with the understanding that each had a right of veto. This rarely occurred, if ever, which shows the consensus, at least at the onset.

This activity did not slow down his legal studies. He became a staff member of the *Journal of the Study of Law* (*Tijdschrift Rechtsgeleerheid*) of which Jacob van Hall, his brother, and Professor Den Tex were the founders and editors.

The Reveil did not totally satisfy Anne Maurits; it was not a religious movement. The opportunity would come soon, however.

In May 1835, he married Suze van Schermbeek. The young couple found a house on the Keizersgracht; it was next to the Wolvenstraat and close to his brother Floris Adriaan.

Suze is the first Van Hall woman about whom we learn something more. Of her predecessors, the wives of old MC and FA in Vianen and the wives of Adriaan and FA in Leiden, we know only that they were good housewives, charming, devout, and brought a large number of children into the world. They did not venture outside and apparently did not write.

Suze was everything these women were and a lot more. Barely nineteen years old at her wedding and already a widow three years later, she left her mark on the Reveil and the Separation (*Afscheiding*). She was a beloved young woman with a steadfast character and a deep religious conviction. We have her religious last will, which was intended for her three young children. She wrote it at the age of twenty-seven, shortly before her death, with a pencil on many sheets of paper. A more beautiful legacy is almost not conceivable.

I don't know if these writings will ever find their way into your hands, however I need to write . . . .

Dear children, I am very sick and I believe that the same illness that took away your beloved Father, now 5 years ago, already soon, may bring your Mother to God . . . .

My Maurits, you look just like your Father, may you share his intelligence and his faith. Oh, I pray that God will bestow on you his faith . . . .

Dear Johanna, sweet and gentle child, agh, yes you will miss your Mother as you grow up. Oh, how my heart beats with joy, when you, my child, wrapped your little arms around my neck and buried your face when I spoke of the Holy Land and you said you loved Him. Oh my daughter, give your heart to the Lord. Oh! May God save you from false lips and the ingratiating tongue! . . .

And you my Floris, child of happiness, child of sorrow [This was because he was born when his father was dying], *oh, my consolation and happiness, often in my most anguishing sorrow, how I often surrendered you as a Samuel to the Lord. Oh! May my prayer be answered and you become a servant of the Lord . . . .*

Farewell! Farewell! I am not able to continue. Almighty God, you know the battle . . . .

Your so deeply loving Mother,
Utrecht 20 December 1843

Mrs. Gerda Kraan-van den Burg gave an outstanding description of her in *Burning Hearts—the History of Maurits and Suze van Hall* [*Brandende Harten—de geschiedenis van Maurits en Suze van Hall*]. Rev. J. Bosch also wrote about her in his book *A Short but Difficult Life—A. M. C. van Hall* [*Een korte maar moeielijk levensdag—A. M. C. van Hall*]. And even in 1954, an article appeared in *Trouw* (a Dutch newspaper) about Suze with the title "Women from the Reveil," which was also written by Mrs. Kraan. Suze was, of course, not the only woman in those circles who drew attention. Among her women friends we find Mrs. Scholte-Brandt, the wife of the famous preacher, and Mrs. De Clercq-Boissevain, who is also a figure of note.

In 1834, in Ulrum, De Cock separated himself from the Reformed Church. Others followed his example, among which were two friends of Maurits, Reverend Scholte and Reverend Budding. He knew Budding from his days in the boarding school in Vianen and the campaign to Belgium.

The government—most of the magistrates were Reformed—regarded the splitting of the national church as an attack on the public order and decided to break it up. An obstacle was article 190 of the constitution, in which the freedom of religion for everybody is guaranteed. It was considered to be no problem; something would be found to overcome it.

The Separatists were, on the whole, simple folks: farmers, fishermen, and workers. They belonged to the least fortunate of the country. Was the hatred for them perhaps caused by social reasons? What right did the masses have to insist that the Reformed magistrates were not following the right path and had to return to the original teachings of the church?

A systematic persecution started, and the government let the "spontaneous" events against the Separatists happen unpunished. They were placed on the blacklist. No one bought from them. On the streets, they were attacked and cajoled. Work was not offered to them, and life was made impossible for their children at school. These negative acts were to no avail; the number of renegades kept growing.

Then an astute jurist found in the Napoleonic Code Pénal an article that forbade twenty or more people from congregating around literary, religious, or political issues. That the constitution had rescinded this provision a long time ago did not matter. The older readers will remember how in the Second World War, the German occupier breathed new life into this provision.

Police posts were positioned in front of the houses and farms of the Separatists. The instant a twenty-first visitor entered, the whole group was arrested and a summons was issued. This continued with a monotonous regularity. Sometimes the fines were established in such a manner that the guilty could not quite pay them, and then the paltry household effects would be auctioned off.

Practically the whole legal community was against the Separatists. Lawyers either could not be found or were found with difficulty. In addition, there rarely was any money to hire a lawyer.

Unless one knocked on the door of Anne Maurits.

With complete conviction, he would take on the defense.

Thus he, on 10 October 1835, presented a case in front of the Provincial Court of Justice in Arnhem. On the remote farm of J. Walraven, which was near Vuren, on 12 July 1835, some people came together for a religious ceremony. Reverend Scholte spoke to them on the farmyard. The court in Tiel fined Scholte, Walraven, and eight other people, against which they filed an appeal with the highest authority, the Provincial Court of Justice in Arnhem. The plea of Van Hall, *In Defense for the Freedom of Religious Practice in the Netherlands*, covered seventy-five pages and was widely distributed in print form. It served as the example in other proceedings, and it earned him the name of Lawyer of the Persecuted Separatists. It is a first-rate piece and was eloquently presented. However, one thing could not be evaded: there were more than twenty people present on the farmyard of the farmer Walraven. The Provincial Court ratified the sentence of the court in Tiel. Reverend Scholte conducted his own defense. In those days, he was very busy because he was successively on trial in Den Bosch, Gorcum, Utrecht, Arnhem, Middelburg, and The Hague. He was sentenced everywhere.

In the meantime, the Ministry of Justice found a new weapon. They sent members of the cavalry (*dragonders*) to maintain public order in the homes of the Separatists, where they were quartered without compensation. In vain Van Hall declared that his clients praying and reading the Bible together in their quiet living rooms did not harm anybody and that it was the dragonders who disturbed the peace. The word *dragonder* still has a bad taste for the Calvinists.

He was very busy as a lawyer. J. F. Gefken, Esq., came to help him, and in the province, other colleagues took on the defense of the Separatists, among whom were Donker Curtius and the Friesian lawyer B. T. Baron van Heemstra; the Van Heemstras never lacked courage.

Van Hall entered the fight as a lawyer and a combatant against injustice. In 1836, he and Suze joined the faith of the Separatists and fell into the ranks of the persecuted brothers.

Reverend Budding played an important role in their conversion. It entailed a profound exploration of the soul, and although Suze initially expressed some hesitation, she joined also.

A storm erupted. This was betrayal of their class. Association with them was shunned. They were assaulted on the streets. Only the Réveil friends and their family stayed loyal.

Father Maurits and Floris looked at this with great concern. This was the end of his career because no one would commission a Separatist. It would be the end of the law office established so many years ago by the old gentleman. The marriage of Floris was childless, and he already had his eye on a political career. The whole office would have thus fallen to Anne Maurits.

They tried to change his mind, but then came the proud answer: "With religion and the truth, there is no compromise possible."

Both men did not give up so easily. They looked for the weakest point in his armor, and they turned to Suze with all their persuasive powers. "Is this really wise? Anne Maurits had, before his marriage, already an attack of TB, and the illness has returned. He exerts himself too much. He has done more than enough for the Separatists. If he continues like this, he won't have long to live." Suze nodded her head. "And then think of your children, the little Maurits and the little one who will arrive in a few months. Why don't you help us?"

Their efforts were to no avail. The little twenty-year-old woman shook her head.

Life in Amsterdam did not offer many opportunities anymore, and they moved to the Veerkade in The Hague. He resigned from the editorial board of *De Stemmen*; his last contribution is called "Something about the Church [*Iets over de Kerk*]."[11]

He immediately found work; he had to plead a case in front of the Provincial Court. In Amsterdam, he had obtained exonerating sentences a couple of times on his plea bargains; in two of the cases, Reverend Scholte was among the accused. Perhaps Father Maurits, the president of the Court of First Appeals, had a hand in it; he was a convinced proponent of freedom of religion, and his authority was at a high point. He did not have the public prosecutor on his side because he appealed the case at the Provincial Court of Holland in Den Haag. The Supreme Court did not exist at that time; after a decision by the Provincial Court of Holland (North Holland and South Holland were one), no further appeal was possible.

---

[11] The anonymity of published articles was no more. The Réveil friends did not support his religious beliefs.

Van Hall prepared his appeal very carefully. So much depended on the verdict.

On 10 October 1836, exactly one year after the judgment in Arnhem, the case was called. The lawyer found a hostile court against him.

He made his plea, but when he came to the end of his speech, the advocate general, Van Appeltere, had a poisonous arrow on his bow.

Van Hall said, "If one deems this preferable for the public tranquility, seemly—"

Van Appeltere jumped up and shouted, "The honorable counselor acts as a public prosecutor against His Majesty, the King!" The president of the Court of Justice also interceded.

It concerned the little word *one*. In other words, it meant the government; in other words, it meant the king. It was public defamation of the King!

The arrow hit the mark. Van Hall, deeply shocked and under protest, brought his defense to a close.

Barbertje (a Dutch expression of someone accused wrongly) must hang. The defendants were sentenced. Also, the Separatists in the province of Holland now did not fall under the protection of the law.

Van Hall, before this, put his faith in King Willem I. He was convinced that the king was not well informed by his advisors and therefore had composed a petition. However, in those days, one could not, just like that, send a petition to the king; one had to initially comply with all kinds of formalities. It went through the mayors and then the governors of the king. The process entailed multiple reviews and thus arrived in the hands of the king four days after the decision of the court.

Nowadays, there are no barriers between the king and the citizens. We recently heard of a heartwarming example. Shortly after the Second World War, a young woman, a descendant of the Separatists, entered a civil marriage. In the meantime, she continued working. The church wedding would have to wait until a house was found. When the first sprout initially announced itself, she was overcome with despair. She wrote a letter to Queen Juliana: "It is all the fault of a lack of housing and now I cannot marry in a white gown." With royal promptness, the Mother of the Fatherland wrote a comforting and invigorating letter. Sometime later, the new citizen of the world appeared in his parental home.

One can understand that the persecution became unbearable for some. So a group of three hundred people from Utrecht left their country, which did not want them, for America. Among them was Hermannus Stulting, one of the better well-off because he had a large furniture workplace near Breukelen, along the river Vecht. His granddaughter Pearl Buck, a winner of the Nobel Prize, described in her book *The Exile* the history of her ancestors, and in its first chapter, she talked about the life of the Stultings in Utrecht. The wife of the author recently had the honor of meeting Pearl Buck in America, and she heard that the expatriates truly did not have an easy time, especially during the years of the Civil War. The parents of Pearl Buck were missionaries in China, and her experience there was the inspiration for *The Good Earth*.

Anne Maurits knew now what to do. First of all, he published his The Hague plea with the title *The Freedom of the Reformed Municipalities in the Netherlands* [*De Vrijheid van de Gereformeerde Gemeenten in Nederland*]. Together with Reverend Scholte and some others, he set up the magazine *De Reformatie* in which the faith was disseminated and the persecutions were excoriated. The fact that the accusations of extensive abuse were founded on the truth became evident when the government never did pursue the editors for defamation. He opened his house for church services. The first time was in October 1836; there were nine people present of whom only three could read. Yet the community expanded quickly. He cried out in Arnhem, "Persecution creates fuel, also like here, where it is missing." In the whole country, there were now eighty thousand Separatists. He became a deacon and an elder.

In January 1837, a police post of two police officers was stationed at his front door. They noted the names of the persons visiting his house. And whenever more than twenty were present, the police forced their way in and wrote tickets. The punishments were fifty guilders and court charges.

The family made sure there was money in the house, but Anne Maurits spent it quickly on fellow believers in need. When, for example, fishermen from Scheveningen were fired because they did not want to work on Sundays, he contributed one thousand guilders to the building of *Bomschuit*—a "pink," a type of flat-bottomed fishing boat for the North Sea—so that they could go out to sea again and earn some money.

Of the old Réveil friends, not all remained faithful to him. Groen van Prinsterer was not allowed by his father to associate with him and he sentenced the followers with a fierce pen. Abraham Capadose became a good friend. We have a small book from the Reverend A. S. Thelwall of Trinity College, Cambridge, one of the men of the Réveil in England. Its title is *Thoughts in Affliction*. Thelwall sent it to Da Costa, who, in turn, gave it to Capadose. The latter gave it to Anne Maurits shortly before his death with this instruction (which was written in English): "With Christian and sympathizing feelings from his brother in the Lord and in afflictions."

In the meantime, the tuberculosis continued its devastating path. Every day he had a fever, but he continued working and did not want to give himself rest.

The doctor prescribed milk from a donkey, but it did not help. Driving horses in an open carriage was the only exercise he had in the end.

The battle became too heavy. On 15 August 1838, the end came.

Capadose and Gefken spelled each other while keeping him company. Father Maurits spent five days next to Anne Maurits; however, when it appeared that the end was not close, he went back to Amsterdam.

The funeral took place with a splendor that did not correspond with the simplicity and soberness that Anne Maurits practiced in the last years of his life.

A long procession of coaches, among which was the coach of Groen, followed the coffin to Eik en Duinen. There were sixteen bearers, in addition to the personal servants of F. A. van Hall and Jacob van Hall, of Kruseman and Dirk van Hogendorp who, dressed in livery, carried the sad burden.

The old father and fourteen brothers and brothers-in-law joined at the grave. There was seen Reverend Scholte; Dudok Bosquet, the only Revéil friend who followed him in the Separation; Capadose; Gefken; and many Separatists of the community of The Hague.

Reverend Budding could not make it; he was in prison in Middelburg.

There were speeches and prayers.

Father Maurits returned to Amsterdam and wrote in his daybook about *"the loss of his magnificent and devout son Anne Maurits Cornelis . . . a magnificent person and Christian."* Yes, the whole family had the highest respect for the fearless fighter although they did not share his beliefs.

Even though her faith was strengthened, the heartbroken widow decided to leave The Hague with her three children—the two-and-a-half-year-old Maurits Cornelis, the one-and-a-half-year-old Hanna, and the couple-of-weeks-old Floris Adriaan—going back to her hometown of Utrecht. Her mother, Helena van Schermbeek, still lived in the large house on the Breestraat together with her brother Willem, who occasionally had sent Suze, living in The Hague, money when she ran short. Nevertheless, she liked to live alone and rented a house on the Weerdsingel, on the corner of the Bemuurde Weerd.

The horrible illness, tuberculosis, touched her too.

She totally immersed herself in her faith. She was popularly called the Protestant Holiness. The Scholtes also live in Utrecht; they were of great support to her.

She died on 27 January 1844—on the day her friend Mrs. Scholte-Brandt was buried. She had reached the age of twenty-seven years old.

We read in *Burning Hearts* that Willem de Clercq, upon hearing of the passing of Suze, wrote the following in his daybook:

> I still see her during the time the roses were in bloom, with her humility and so much courage, in the distress of the first illness of Van Hall, in the distress of their parting, in the difficulties of the first move to The Hague, in the long suffering of the illness, in the isolating first days in Utrecht. She had a degree of loyalty, a degree of sincerity that I have found in only a few people. Her remembrance is a blessing. The memory of her course in life and her victories enlivened us.

A few days later, Willem de Clercq passed away.

After the return to Amsterdam from the funeral, old Maurits had to fulfill a task. He already had copies of Suze's farewell letter to her children made. He also had copies made of the poems he composed for the three orphans in which he encouraged them to follow the example of their parents. The pieces were bound in three commemorative booklets, and Suze, just before her death, gave them to her children.

Now his thoughts went to the just-deceased Willem de Clercq, one of the most trusted friends of Anne Maurits and Suze. He did not write what he then did in his own daybook, but we found it in the daybook of Gideon Jeremie Boissevain, the great-grandfather on the mother's side of this author; Caroline, the daughter of Gideon, was married to Willem de Clercq.

Here we give the word to Gideon Boissevain:

Monday, 12 February. Met with Mister M. C. van Hall who requested an audience; we sat for ¾ hour and had a most important discussion with his Eminence about the interests of Caroline and her children. His Eminence had had dinner with His Majesty. The King and the Crown Prince and more specifically the Queen had wholeheartedly inquired with interest about the circumstances in which Caroline found herself. His Eminence had recommended that Gerrit should often come to the Palace of Justice and diligently continue his studies.

I asked M. C. van Hall his perspective about the discourse of the poems and notes of de Clercq.

Received visits from Professor van Lennep, from Dykveld, Esq., and Jer. de Vries. In the evening visited Caroline and informed her about the communications of M. C. van Hall.

Tuesday, 13 February. In the morning at 9 o'clock informed Gerrit what M. C. van Hall had communicated.

Friday, 16 February. A visit to His Excellency of the State Council D. J. van Ewyck about Jan Pieterzoon Koen. Discussed Caroline de Clercq and her sons and urged the desirable outcome if the Trading Company took care of the widow.

It went well with Gerrit. He, among other things, became a member of the state council.

Maurits Cornelis van Hall, Esq., 1836–1900

This then was the story about our ancestors, about whom we started the book. We understand now that the Reformed press did not think it was right that these ancestors of Mayor Gijsbert van Hall were not mentioned.

Anne Maurits did not become, as his father and brothers, a secretary of state, nor did he become a professor or a president of the court of justice or a baron or what have you. Suze and he fought for religion and love of one's fellow man. What more can one long for?

The three young orphans were raised in Utrecht by Aunt Van Schermbeek. There were no financial difficulties. Did the commemorate booklets of Grandfather Maurits make an impact on the children? We doubt that. In both families, there existed only one major fear: that the children would get into contact with the Separatists/Calvinists; they were also afraid that they would catch a cold and then get tuberculosis. Therefore they wore thick underwear and knit woolen shawls, under which this writer had to pay the penalty too. The oldest son, the above-mentioned Maurits Cornelis, heard for the first time from his costudents in Utrecht that something untoward had happened to his parents. And when the mother of the author, Hester Boissevain (who made her entry into the household of her fiancé Jan van Hall around 1893), asked with interest about the grandparents, Anne Maurits and Suze, the prospective mother-in-law answered her with "Hester, about those people we don't speak of in this house!" This made Hester Boissevain curious, and she asked the children of the house if they could enlighten her. They whispered, "They were in jail! Perhaps they were alcoholics or something like that."

It was 1853. The elderly but mentally totally aware grandfather Maurits sat in his study on the Herengracht with his leg, which had been bothering him, elevated.

He was the undisputed head of the family. The Van Halls had always recognized the patriarchy rather than the matriarchy. One could not underestimate the power that came from that. Among each other, they differed in opinions, but to the outside, there was a united front.

He was waiting for his son Floris, who announced his visit from The Hague.

Close ties bound father and son; for years they worked together in their law office. In age, they differed only twenty-three years, and one could have described their relation as one between an older brother and a younger one. When Floris went to live in The Hague, he kept his father abreast of all the events through writing. We found a brief letter in which Floris related that he started his secretary-of-state position; he wrote this at seven o'clock in the morning in his new office. His first task was a letter to his father. (Nowadays, the secretary of state arrives a bit later!)

This was eleven years ago. Ever since then, Floris received many political and legal suggestions and advice from his father and also from his brother Jacob, the scholar who perhaps was the smartest in the family. According to the family, it was evident that Floris very much missed their support after these advisors died.

In his political career, Floris remained always a lawyer. His strength lay in achieving a compromise in which others never saw an opportunity. He lacked the one-track thinking of Thorbecke or Groen van Prinsteren. He swerved between what the circumstances demanded to the left or the right.

Floris formed, as the successor of Thorbecke, a new department.

What happened? Pope Pius IX announced in March that one archbishop and four bishops would settle in the Netherlands. The constitution of 1848 gave him that right—a right that Thorbecke acknowledged. This caused much agitation among the Protestants—a time known in the history books as the April Movement of 1853 (*Aprilbeweging van 1853*). In Amsterdam, riots threatened to break out. Under this pressure, Thorbecke stood down.

Then everything happened at a fast pace. On 16 April, Floris accepted the assignment, and on 20 April, a cabinet was formed.

To have more freedom during the discussions of the Ministerial Council, he sent Lichtenvelt, the secretary of state for the Roman Catholic Worship, with a message for the pope to Rome. It was a long journey during those days. Floris, on a temporary basis, took on the duties of the Roman Catholic Worship.

Groen van Prinsterer and Professor Royaards gave him advice, and thus came into being the Religion Law—Van Hall (*Godsdienstwet—Van Hall*), which is still in force in large measure today. The law regulates the oversight of the

1787 Princes Wilhelmina at the Goejanverwellessluis.
Collectie Atlas van Stolk.

Joyfull entrance of Lodewijk Napoleon into Amsterdam (Amstelstraat)
Collectie Atlas van Stolk.

1813, The Cossacks bivouacking outside the gates of Amsterdam.
Collectie Atlas van Stolk.

respective church societies. The provisions apply to the churches evenly; there seemingly is no discrimination. The Protestants are not pleased that the law forbids the right of procession and states that church dignitaries cannot claim privileges and positions, such as the pontifical title of prince of the Holy Blood (prins van den Bloede).

The unrest calmed down, and the constitution remained in place. Shortly thereafter, the bishops were appointed.

While Maurits awaited Floris, his thoughts turned to the past.

If this law had existed during the times of Anne Maurits, then there would not have been trouble with gatherings of more than twenty people. *But then,* he thought, *the courts would have found something else.* Moreover, King Willem II already gave the Separatists the freedom to practice their religion some years ago. It had to be this way.

The law office of Van Hall ceased to exist. Floris became a politician, and now his best years were coming. Thorbecke, the liberal with dangerous ideas, had to clear the field for him.

Moreover, the occasion was, for grandfather Maurits (the proponent of religious freedom), not very sympathetic. Not one member of the Van Hall family signed any of the numerous petitions against the Catholics. One was either the patriarch or not.

There was a knock on the door. Floris entered. He enthusiastically talked about the latest events in The Hague, but that was not the real reason why he came.

Already eight years a widower, he had found a woman who wanted to marry him. She was Lady Henriëtte Schimmelpenninck van der Oye, Dame du Palais and the first lady-in-waiting (*grootmeesteres*) of Princess Hendrik; she was twenty-six-years old.

Maurits looked at his son. It was quite a difference in age. The groom was sixty-two, though still in the vigor of his life. He was tall, graying, and with an exceptional charm. Didn't he capture the heart of this beautiful foreign actress in one day? During that time, wasn't that precious pearl necklace of good use? Maurits gave his permission, although from a legal point of view, this was not necessary anymore.

Then they talked about their godchildren, Maurits and Floris, who, as young orphans, we left behind in the previous chapter. They were seventeen and fourteen years old.

In any case, studying law was the conclusion. Then there were so many opportunities also in the financial field. The Netherlands, after all, was at the brink of a tremendous industrial and colonial expansion.

So it came to pass.

The two young men founded banks, and their sister Hanna also became involved in the financial world. She married Johan Gleichman (who was nicknamed the Gray Top Hat), the right hand of Secretary of State Floris in 1860. He joined the management of the Netherlands Bank, became the secretary of state for finances, and then became the secretary of state for the state.

To the dismay of the old patriarch Maurits and their uncle Floris, their godchildren became liberals and followers of Thorbecke! In those times in the conservative circles, it was the equivalent to an illness like leprosy. One really did not want to associate with them. Within the family, it did not matter.

In 1865, we find the young Maurits in Amsterdam as the secretary of the Crediet- en Depositobank and married to Debora Cremer Eindhoven, who was of northern blood (she was a Friesian and from Groningen). We are not very proud of that. Throughout the years, Amsterdam attracted from the north new blood, people with entrepreneurial spirit and fresh ideas. There were many, many people whose last names ended with -*ma*, -*stra*, or -*da*. Friesland did supply half of the police force and even two Amsterdam mayors, Sjoerd Vening Meinesz and Feike de Boer. The top of the province Overijsel brought us the lineage of the Goedkoops. The provinces of Groningen and Drente, however, stayed behind. The magnet of Amsterdam pulled them all in.

Rotterdam has drawn more from the people reservoir from the southern islands; the people there are a more conservative group than the ones in the north. Amsterdam consequently has always been more left oriented.

After the liquidation of the Crediet- en Depositobank, Maurits contributed to the establishment of the Succ. de la Banque de Paris et des Pays-Bas. One of the sons of King Willem III gave his support to it. Mijnhart Boissevain and Maurits became directors, and the head office was established on the Herengracht 539, the old office of the Crediet- en Depositobank.

It was not correct to still call him by his first name, Maurits; that would have been too familiar. He had become a distinguished patriarch—a real one—with a long, dark beard. The family called him Papa Van Hall and later called him Opa Van Hall. He lived with his family of nine children on the bend of the Herengracht, Nr. 475. It is now the office of the Dutch Society of Life Insurance (*Hollandse Sociëteit van Levensverzekeringen*). A. E. d'Ailly, a former mayor of Amsterdam, called it one of the most representative patrician houses from previous centuries. On the outside, it already stands out with its rich architecture; inside, one will find in the stairwell, hallways, vestibule, and paneling an overwhelming luxury from different art periods—murals by Moucheron and Jurriaan Andriessen, sculptures by Husley and Logteren, and ceiling paintings by De Witt and De Lairesse.

From this house strode Papa Van Hall every day, the symbol of the classic-liberal banker with a walking stick with a silver haft in his hand, benignly greeting his acquaintances with a nod of his top hat as he walked to his office at Nr. 539. It was on the quiet Herengracht on which no cars or bicycles obstructed traffic, only the occasional carriage. The pedestrians leisurely strolled along there because the clothing did not permit anything else. The ladies dressed in long black overcoats and bonnets; the servants, in aprons and caps.

On the opposite side of the canal—the even-numbered side—lived, among others, S. P. van Eeghen, J. Luden, Insinger-van Loon, Barnouw, Van Lennep, and not to forget, Mayor Vening Meinesz, who lived at Nr. 456. This number had a particular meaning for one of the daughters of the family home. Hanna van Hall married his son Sjoerd. The courting did not occur as freely as in the days of Adriaan van Hall, who told us of his experience on the island of Terschelling. No, it took place via a third person, the sister of the young Sjoerd. Coba Vening Meinesz and Hanna communicated for hours, one sitting in the window of Nr. 475 and the other sitting in the window on the opposite side of the canal, through sign language with their fingers.

The courting took place in this way. They lived in the Victorian period.

In the bend of the Herengracht, big parties were organized.

We now take our readers along to a wedding in the house of Van Hall; in particular, it was the wedding of Jan, one of the sons of the house and the father of the author, and Hester, the daughter of Charles Boissevain, the director and editor in chief of the newspaper *Algemeen Handelsblad*.

Jan van Hall, or "Unze Jan" as he was colloquially called in Amsterdam, lived already for a number of years in Baltimore in the United States of America, where he had established a timber company. In January 1895, he returned from America for the wedding.

The series of celebrations began on 20 February 1895 with a dinner commemorating the official registration of the coming marriage at the Herengracht 475.

The guests rode to the front of the house. They entered the house through the front door above the sidewalk, which had the double stairs (if there was no party, the entrance below was used). The big white entry hall was lit by candles and lanterns. A servant announced in a loud voice the guests. There one could see the parents of the bride with nine of their eleven children and numerous Boissevains, among whom was Nel, the future mother of Mayor Gijsbert. Of Mama's family, one could see the Cremer Eindhovens, Gerard Vissering, and Fabius. There was Uncle Johan Gleichman, the Krusemans, the Den Texens, and the Van Eeghens.

In the dining room were fifty-two place settings.

The reader should not be startled by the menu. Twelve courses! Soup, canapés, fish, venison, veal chops, bone marrow with celery, pheasants! For a moment, we will leave the table to catch our breath. Then we will go full steam ahead: lobster, cold chicken, paté de foie gras, ice cream, cake, and dessert! The five or six wines were not mentioned on the menu; this would become the custom later. It is obvious that the cellar of the host was well filled with fine wines, which were imported by the barrel. The wine was thus not poured out of bottles but out of crystal carafes that were placed between the candles, which created a sparkling and festive atmosphere. The meal lasted till deep in the night.

On 22 February, there was an intimate dinner at the Van Tienhovens; fourteen people attended.

On 24 February, a Sunday, there was a reception at the bride's house. It was unbelievably busy on the Herengracht for Nr. 332. Carriages arrived and left. Later the exuberant youth ran up and down the two stairways, through the garden, around the chicken shed, and back into the house. Mayor Vening Meinesz mumbled, "Next time, I am bringing my constables along!"

The next day, the young couples Boissevain-Pijnappel and Van Eeghen–Boissevain invited guests to a *soirée dansant*. They did not have large houses, and so the party was held at Riche on the Rokin. As our female friend, who we have invited, does not have to her avail a carriage, a porter will accompany her, for a quarter, to the party. Under no circumstances may our young friend do anything else. In the meantime, as Jan had never been to the house of his hosts and hostesses, he paid them, while in his official attire, a visit. In doing so, he held his gloves tightly in his left hand. Perhaps Jan had the luck that no one was home and he only had to leave his business card. The proprieties after the party could not be forgotten.

After arriving in the banquet halls of Riche while dressed in dress coats and patent leather shoes, male guests greeted the host and hostess, and then they went from young woman to young woman. One would first bow deeply and ask if a lady still had a dance available. The dance cards would be compared, and then one could note, with the elegant pencil in his gleaming white glove, her name. For a moment, he would hold his heart, but yes, his favorite, surrounded by young men, had kept the festive supper of nine courses open for him.

The grand ball started. First was the Polonaise, and then followed all those old-fashioned dances: the Pas de Patineurs, the Quadrille des Lanciers, the Mazurka, the Tempête, the Waltz, the Kruispolka, and the Polka. "O, mijn lieve zwart kop, o, mijn lieve zwart kop!" The guests would return very late home.

On 27 February, there was a dinner with Uncle Niek and Aunt Hes den Tex-Boissevain; twenty-four guests attended. There was also a play and ballet.

On 2 March, there was a great ball and performance at Mr. and Mrs. Jacob P. Boissevain's place. We will see here a few new faces: H. Teixeira de Mattos, Van Barneveld Kooy, J. C. and H. W. van Marle, P. Tegelberg, C. M. Uytenbogaard, E. Bicker, R. D. Buma, Van Eibergen Santhagens, C. van Lennep, B. Hooglandt, M. A. von Hemert, and D. Op ten Noort. There was a dinner of six courses.

The next day, there was an afternoon tea at Parkweg Nr. 71.

The following evening, there was a ball at the house of Jan.

At last, on 7 March, the wedding was held in the Walenkerk.

The menu of the wedding lunch at Herengracht 332 was described in a poem by Charles Boissevain. It is as follows:

Wedding Meal of Jan van Hall
  and
Hester Boissevain

7 March 1895

"Give now especially
Something that tastes good
To the great number
Of our wedding friends!"

Then the wife said: "I will
Give first of all
CONSOMMÉ ROYAL
He will find that
Quite delicious!"

No trifle, woman! . . . That is impolite,
Such nothing when at one o'clock you are hungry
And give such a dainty, colorless snack
To the Bride and Groom!

Then she said: "Don't be so bossy,
Your wife is thorough and not a fool;
She therefore gives you FILLET OF BEEF
WITH DELICIOUS VEGETABLES!"

Do not stubbornly persist.
But give and take.
In this manner one mixes gently
The cold and the hot.

Born in Doorn, raised along the Amstel,
On crest of the dunes, warmed by the sea breeze,
Hester kept her eyes to the West and the ocean
The soft expectations from there made her free.
Then he came, took the heart and the hand
Of the pure and beautiful rose of the dunes of the country.
Honoring, appreciating, politely offering
The oceans to the twosome THESE BLUSHING LOBSTERS.

Look, one adorns the house with flowers and green
Because the delightful day has arrived.
And with BUDS OF ASPERGES IN A CREAM WHITE FEAST
Makes us dream of Bussink in the spring.
Oh, CHICLAIR IMPERIAL as the dish is called—his honor!
And when it disappears, because beauty is fragile!
Then this dream again belongs to the past!

Oh lark risen high in the blue.
What do you see the sweetest in the meadow and roads?
I call the sweetest that I found:
CHARLOTTES A LA DEMIDOFF.

Oh quick swallow, announcer of spring,
What does the dear bride need?
Symbol of the sweets in home and courtyard:
CHARLOTTES A LA DEMIDOFF.

Nothing can dissuade Dutch people
To resist at parties
Old fashioned Cheese!
Still we need to keep up with the fashion!
Therefore one prepares for banquets
Tea biscuits to be dipped in melted cheese,
They call it "fromaas PAILETTEN."
You are welcome to your "fromaas"
I choose Gouda Cheese.

After a short honeymoon, the somewhat-tired bride and groom departed by steamer for America.

In the meantime, to catch our breath, we will depart with you readers for the cure in Karlsbad.

All these parties were not only for fun. They were occasions for the youth, under the supervision of the elders, to meet and get to know each other. From a wedding, after all, comes another wedding! J. C. van Marle found his Coba Vening Meinesz. Aat van Hall, a brother of the groom Jan, found his Nel Boissevain,[12] and when one thinks of the great number of children of the Boissevains, the Van Tienhovens, and the related families, there awaited many weddings, and then there were the copper, silver, and gold anniversaries; we need to repeat many times the trip to Karlsbad.

For each Boissevain wedding, the *Algemeen Handelsblad* newspaper, aside from the advertisements and regular columns, devoted an edition totally to each wedding couple.

Had it become a happy marriage? Yes. We can read about it in a work that was written twelve and a half years later; it was written in honor of the copper anniversary of Jan and Hester, which was celebrated in the Frankhuis near Zwolle. In the Zwolle edition of 7 September 1907, Charles Boissevain wrote in his column, "From Day to Day," the following:

> *"What does to love mean anyway, Grandfather?" asked Johnnie van Hall about a year and a half ago when we were walking through the pine trees in Drafna. He asked me occasionally such questions, which always make me almost slither on the slippery pine needles!*

> *I believe I sort of answered as follows: "Well, if you find that your life is warmer, richer, happier, fuller, purer, more musical, and full of hope when you are near a person . . . that you are happier when you sit next to someone like that, rather than walking through the pines trees with me, then you love somebody."*

> *"But Grandfather, I am very happy now, because I like it here."*

---

[12] Mr. C. F. van Maanen, the Minister of Justice from 1814 to 1842, was responsible for the persecution of Anne Maurits and the Separatists. His daughter, Mrs. Brugmans-Van Maanen, was the grandmother of Nel Boissevain. When she heard of the engagement of Aat and Nel, she sent a message from The Hague that said that Aat should come for a visit as fast as possible. "This is the moment," she said, "when the two families make up." It did not happen. When Aat arrived in The Hague and rang the bell, he heard that Mrs. Brugmans just had an attack from which she shortly after died.

"Thank you Johnnie, that proves you also love me a little. But with whom do you love to be the most with?"

"With Father and Mother in the Cabin?" (Our wooden vacation cabin near Hulshorst.)

"Now Johnnie, that proves that you love your father and mother and the cabin the most!"

"No, that is not true! I love Freddie much more than the Cabin!"

"There you are, now you know what to love is!" I said wiping off the sweat on my forehead.

Not only Johnnie, but a large number of people have learned what it is to love their parents. They feel happy to be in their presence. They never think about which great qualities differentiate them or how handsome and charming and wise they are. No, they are happy in their presence.

That is all . . . but that is immense. One trusts them . . . one is sure of their loyalty and their good thoughts toward them.

When I am in that warm, affectionate and dear home of Jan and Hes, I feel embraced by many invisible ties. A father, who looks at his daughter in the living room, who herself is busy, surrounded by many children, suddenly sometimes sees in front of him twenty daughters Hester. He sees her as a baby . . . as a timid young girl . . . as an adorable little sister of her two smaller sisters Olga and Hilda . . . as a young girl in Zandvoort . . . as a happy woman . . . as a worshipped mother. And in those little daughters Hester has something of her mother, now a glance, then a laugh, then a movement, then a simplicity, who can be as happy in a cabin as in a palace, then a firm deportment with difficulties and sorrow, then an always soft warmth of love bestowing tenderness and selflessness.

Maurits Cornelis van Hall, Esq., Heer van Heicop en Boeicop,
1768 – 1858, 87 years old.
Next to him his oldest son Floris Adriaan Baron van Hall, Esq.,
1791 – 1866.
Below his sons Dr. Jacob van Hall, Esq., 1799 – 1859 and Prof. Dr. H. C. van Hall,
1801 – 1874.

Anne Maurits Cornelis van Hall, Esq., 1808 – 1838
Suze van Hall van Schermbeek 1816-1844
"Blessed are the dead, who die in the arms of the Lord" Openb. XIV – 13

Fourth House from the left, Keizersgracht 289, where Maurits and Suze lived
during their first years.

EENE KERMISPRENT,

WAAROP WORDT VOORGESTELD

HET DROEVIG RELAAS DER MISERIEN

OP EENE REIS VAN

GEESTELIJKE LANDVERHUIZERS

NAAR

Een boer en boerin van 75 jaar
gaan in Amerika sterven. lou-
ter uit verandering.

Spot en hoon begeleidden de vervolgde Afgescheidenen ook op hun reis naar de Verenigde
Staten van Amerika.

Collectie Atlas van Stolk.

Mockery and scorn accompanied the persecuted Separatists
on their voyage to the United States of America.
Collectie Atlas van Stolk

Ballet in honor of the newly weds Jan van Hall and Hester Boissevain in 1895.
The costumes were made of black and red satin, the colors of Amsterdam. Left
to right Aat van Hall, Olga Boissevain (later van Stockum), Rutger Jan Boissevain,
Hilda Boissevain (later de Booy), Jo Boissevain (later van Hemert), Errie
Ankersmit, Henk van den Berg, Hanna van Hall (later Vening Meinesz).

Yes Johnnie, I know what it is to love . . . what it is to love his daughter and her husband and family.

I always feel so warm, so fortunate, so cheerful and young in their presence.

May God Almighty bless that beloved family throughout the long joyful years!

We once asked an old uncle what the situation was *with finances in those times and how* much it really cost to live. He gave us the following answer:

Let us assume that Papa Van Hall had an income of around ninety thousand guilders a year. Out of that, he had to pay about five thousand guilders in taxes. Life in the house on the Herengracht and the two country estates cost perhaps thirty thousand guilders or perhaps thirty-five thousand guilders, so about fifty thousand guilders were left to invest in new ventures.

It was the golden age for investments.

In his youth, the author came upon a stock in a small Indonesian company that his father inherited from Papa Van Hall. "Look," said Father Jan, "Opa at that time paid one thousand guilders for it, and as long as I have it, I receive two and a half thousand guilders as a dividend. That is a veritable annual income for a commoner." Thoughtfully he drew on his ever-present cigar. We knew there was more to come. "My eight children must not think they will inherit much from me. Change is in the near future. Taxes will further shrink income and capital. I gave you a good-as-possible upbringing. That should give you an advantage, but for the rest, you have to care for yourself." These are wise words that the author herewith passes on to his children.

Outside of his blissful family life and his banking business, Papa Van Hall had few interests. The family spent the summer in Baarn or at Groenendaal, near Hulshorst. Groenendaal originally was owned by the Cremer Eindhovens. There they could escape the wet and damp Friesland/Overijsel for the high, dry, and sandy soil. It was an extensive country estate with the usual sand drifts. Our little wooden vacation house, "de Hut," still stands, but the sand drifts, which could be seen out of the windows of a train, Father Jan transferred "the Hut" to Piet van Tienhoven of the Nature Conservation (*Natuurmonumenten*). The railways complained that the sand covered the rails, and it cost the family more and more money. Now the Natuurmonumenten has to attend to it, and we may walk freely as much as in the past. The actual cause for the transfer was a tempting offer by the municipality of The Hague to turn it into a garbage dump. A shiver went through the family. That beautiful piece of nature, of which so many cherished memories were associated with, a garbage dump? Never. And to circumvent that, one would change their mind sometime later. It was declared a nature conservation.

Papa Van Hall also did something in politics. He was a member of the Provincial States of North Holland and, from 1896 to 1900, a member of the First Chamber.

Was he a combative figure, this grandchild of the patriot Maurits Cornelis and son of Anne Maurits? We looked up the proceedings of the Chamber, and though he was always present, he never uttered a word. Well, he could not because he had cancer in his throat and could only breathe through a silver tube that was placed in his trachea.

Why did he become a member of the Chamber? The family believes that this was tied to the fact that his brother Floris Adriaan discredited the name Van Hall time and time again. His friends believed that something had to be done about this, and to prove to the outside world that Papa Van Hall had their trust, they made him a member of the First Chamber. Undoubtedly he could offer useful written advice on financial matters. He stood outside of the growing social turbulence during those days.

His brother Floris Adriaan and a cousin established in Utrecht the private bank Van Schermbeek & Van Hall. For twelve years, he was a member of the City Council, and it appeared he would follow a normal career. After the death of his wife Christina Jongeneel—the marriage was childless—he spent more time in Amsterdam. He kept his house in Utrecht. It was called the Haunted House Van Hall due to the secretive corridors and the heavy, vaulted doors behind which there was nothing; they were all built to lead burglars astray.

In Amsterdam, he lived in the Palace of People's Industry (*Paleis van Volksvlijt*). We paid him a visit there around 1922. We visited him because we were short of cash, but it was also done partly out of curiosity. Author Bob Boissevain had namely mentioned that after his engagement to Sonja van Tienhoven, he paid a courtesy call to her great uncle Floris, who, after rooting around in his safe, presented him with a thousand-guilder banknote as a wedding present!

We were not allowed to visit him during the day as he slept then. He could not bear the daylight, and that was why he arose around seven o'clock in the evening and went to bed in the morning. He also feared open spaces. Everyone had to accommodate themselves to his hours, to the astonishment and inconvenience of his tenants in Friesland, who he made to appear at his hotel in the middle of the night.

While somewhat embarrassed, we once reported during an evening to the ticket booth of the Glass Palace. The public was already streaming in, and we were not able to buy a ticket. The concierge nevertheless promptly brought me upstairs, and there we found the old uncle just starting his breakfast. Insofar we remember, there were no windows in the room. A door to the left led to a side balcony from which we could view the opera on the stage! This was another benefit. Much more interesting than the singing was the fascinating stories of Uncle Floris. With a soft and civilized voice, he painted a strange and adventurous world in front of our eyes. He talked about theaters, opera companies, famous actors and actresses, silver mines in Central America, the railway concession that enabled the direct line from Amsterdam to Rotterdam, his stay in the Balkans during the Russo-Turkish War, and his friendship with the King of Montenegro. He showed us the Medal of Daniëlo, which the King had given him.

We decided in advance not to dare discuss the difficulties and fate of the Paleis van Volksvlijt, of which he was the President-Commissioner. But he told with relish about the nine months he was jailed in preventive custody in 1899; he then was cleared. He was too smart for all of them. He had strictly followed the law.

He told stories till deep in the night; the performance had already ended a long time ago when suddenly, there was a knock on the door. A gentleman entered and looked suspiciously at me. He kept standing, apparently expecting me to leave. Great Uncle Floris stood up and made his way to the safe. The tension rose, and then came a note of twenty-five guilders, which I quickly placed in my billfold. The nocturnal visitor was visibly relieved. He was one of the swindlers, who, because he was so much smarter than the old uncle, was able to steal to the last cent of the millions he had acquired with so much difficulty.

Since the author Multatuli wrote about the Van Hall chaps (Hallemannetjes) who were so exceptionally proper, the younger members of the family, especially those in high school, were teased about this.

But still he did not use our family as an example.

He was friends with M. C. van Hall Azn and his German mistress. Thus he was not so exceptionally well-behaved! This MC was a cousin and a namesake of Opa Van Hall. In October 1861, Multatuli wrote a letter to his wife, Tine, who found herself then in Brussels; he described an evening he had spent with M. C. van Hall Azn.

Dear finest heart,

The general public does not understand the Love Letters. About four days ago I dined with a Mr. Van Hall (a cousin of the Secretary of State who is married to a freule Schimmelpenninck v.d.O.) who lives with a mistress, a German. The cause of the invitation was through M.H. (author Max Havelaar), but the Love Letters she had not yet read. I sent her an example. The next day I received a letter, (it is in German). I will send it to you. Try to read it, then you will see that this poor German girl, a mistress!, immediately understood much better the depth and scope, than the mean trivial stupid Dutch public. She echoes the melancholy, she feels at any rate the deep grief that gives it air!, and the Reading Society—"Leeskabinet"—, that by the way is for me, says that in the Love Letters are such nice stories!

Oh, I am so sad!

The little piece of the German girl is somewhat wild, a little schwärmerisch, but it shows in any case that she understands grief and those stupid Dutch people talk about nice stories.

I would like it so much if you write her a letter. But to write it for you, I will not. If after reading her little piece you have no feeling in your heart to write her, but I think yes! She is very sensitive and weighed down by her position; a warm word from you to prove that her sympathy is appreciated by you and me, will do her well. I think she has earned it. She will have the same heartfelt feelings as you. I don't have any words for my disgust with the Dutch people, they are cows!

I would like to help you with that letter to the little girl, but I am tired.

With that, the ancestors of our readers made do. And then our family, with the help of the mistress, was shown in a better light!

Multatuli—together with M. C. van Hall Azn, J. Spree, and Raedt van Oldenbarneveldt—had a *Beerclub*. In the memoirs of Mr. d'Ablaing van Giesenberg, the publisher of Multatuli, we read the following description of the beer evenings.

On a certain evening conversing with his friends at Schwab (a pub), he (Multatuli) showed a pronounced restlessness. One asked what bothered him. "What bothers me," he hollered jumping up, "I need music." "Then there is nothing else to do, but that we now go to the Nes," said Readt van Oldenbarnevelt, "because at this hour, almost midnight, all concerts have ended." "Well then, onward to the Nes," said Dekker (AKA Multatuli). The clock struck twelve o'clock when Dekker, Raedt, M. C. van Hall Azn and J. Spree entered the lounge of the "Parlement" and ordered a cup of coffee. To their consternation the musicians were packing up their instruments and it cost those that just entered quite a lot of effort to convince them to do their best on a piece of music. Dekker listened attentively, and the music positively influenced him, as he appeared to be in a calmer mood. When the music quieted down, per local custom, one of the lady performers came to the gentlemen with a small cup. Raedt threw in ten cents. "Give me your wallet," said Dekker who sat next to him, "I don't have any money with me." Raedt guilelessly handed his wallet over, and was astonished when he saw Dekker dump the contents of his wallet in the small cup, seventeen guilders and a few cents, while he sharply added to the owner: "There, you merchants have no appreciation for the arts, realize that you are just a miserable tobacco dealer and she is an artist." Raedt was so upset that he could not answer. Seemingly calm he went to the bar and gave his watch as a temporary guarantee, as he had no money to pay the his and Dekker's bill, but when and wherever after that evening, someone asked if he personally was acquainted with Dekker, he gave air to his indignation, with the statement how immoderate Dekker was with his wallet on that particular night at the Parlement. Raedt, Van Hall and Spree have died, but the daughter of Raedt still lives and she can attest that she heard her father on numerous occasions relate the story.

Meanwhile, bitter poverty prevailed in the slums of Amsterdam. The previously mentioned families willingly participated in philanthropy. Too often though this was just like a drop of water on a hot metal plate.

Still some practical institutions became permanent through their initiatives. An example is the hospital-church ship *De Hoop*. In 1898, Charles Boissevain wrote in his column, "Van Dag tot Dag," in the *Algemeen Handelsblad* about the distress of the fishermen. His future son-in-law, the young naval lieutenant H. de Booy, told him about his experiences on the North Sea on board the fast police-sailing vessel *Argus*. The Hospital Church Ship Association *De Hoop* has been able to keep up with the social evolution during the last sixty years. Starting as an incidental philanthropy, *De Hoop* has become a functional part, the mother ship, of the fishing fleet. It has become ingrained in the consciousness of the Dutch population. From the beginning the following were as chairmen / vice chairmen: E. N. Rahusen, W. Boissevain, Gerard Vissering, Chr. Beels, H. de Booy, M. F. van Lennep, H. L. van Eeghen, Ernst Crone, and the author of this book.[13]

---

[13] The late Queen Mother Emma, at the founding of the association, directed a letter to one hundred women that requested they annually collect one hundred guilders for *De Hoop*. Queen Wilhelmina and Queen Juliana frequently visited the ship. Princess Beatrix continues this tradition. She made a trip on the North Sea together with Princess Irene and some classmates. On the ocean, a demonstration showed how a patient from a fishing boat was transferred to *De Hoop*. Two children of the author, Michael and Ellen, were on board a boat of the Royal North and South Holland Life Saving Company where the emergency signal, two flags, was raised. The hospital-church ship steamed to the boat; quickly a rubber boat was launched. After a couple of moments, the patient, strapped to an iron stretcher, was delivered to the hospital ship. With great suspense, we awaited the reaction of Princess Beatrix, but she was totally dissatisfied. Her words left no doubt what she meant. "When one of the sailors slips on that dancing raft, then the patient on that iron stretcher will inevitably sink to the bottom of the ocean. It is irresponsible." She was right. The gentleman Verhoef in Aalsmeer ingeniously constructed a floating stretcher on which patients could be entrusted without any danger.

HATTEM AND AMSTERDAM

We have followed the adventures of the family through the times of the Regents, as patriots, during the French period, since the beginning of the Kingdom, as Separatists, and during the classic-liberal period.

This is not to say that we, by putting a stripe under the chapters, have finished with the then-prevalent opinions. The different upheavals in the rural areas occurred with a slower tempo than in the big cities. Much of the old remained.

A typical example of that is Hattem, where the author, in his early youth, shortly after the turn of the century, came to live.

Life in Hattem looked a lot like that of Vianen in the seventeenth and eighteenth centuries. Hattem, though, has never had a lord. The citizens were free farmers who entrenched themselves behind walls meters thick for seven centuries. The farms lay behind these walls. The sprawling floodplains along the river IJsel, where the cattle grazed and where the hay must have come from, were communal property named the Homoet or Hoenswaard.

The striking personality of Ph. J. Baron van Heemstra, who was the mayor of Hattem till 1926, put an exceptional stamp on the little city. He was a tall man; white hair; a long, small white beard; a sharp, aristocratic nose; a terrific, loud voice; and a heart of gold.

Much of the life of the city took place on the Church Square (*Kerkplein*); it was surrounded by the seventeenth-century city hall, the post office, the big church, the school of Master Van Zuilen, and let us not forget, the large house of the mayor. One could often see him sitting next to a window, keeping a vigilant look at the square. The moment he saw an acquaintance with whom he wanted to talk, he stepped outside. How often did we hear him holler, "Boy, come *here*! Cap *off*!" When a stranger dared to come to the Church Square, he strode outside with his "rooster walk"—he raised his knees up high—and then his voice blared out to the little village policeman, "Borreman, who is that?" This happened once in 1903 when two canvassers of the SDAP (*Social Democratic Labor Party*) came from Holland to distribute a political pamphlet. Mayor Van Heemstra took one look at the pamphlet and ordered Borreman to set the two men outside the gates of the city.

"But, Mayor, the Constitution gives us the right to do this," they indignantly said.

"I detest your Constitution. Get out!"

And so they went, and for now, they did not come back.

Hattem was, after all, absolutely not ready yet for the SDAP. That happened a number of years later, when the director of the post office, W. H. Baron van Ittersum (a liberal married to Lady Röell), entered as the extreme left-wing element into the Council.

The post office was run good-naturedly. There were nine telephone numbers. On Sundays the post office was closed; however, if we had to telephonically make contact with our friends under special circumstances, then a number of connections were plugged in. The ringer of the old-fashioned telephones rang all at the same time, which caused confusing conversations of Babylonian proportions!

Van Heemstra did not recognize secretaries of state and departments. The Queen had appointed him, and he was only accountable to Her.

This the author noticed in 1919, shortly after he passed his final exams at the Latin section of his high school.

On the Church Square, the mayor saw me. A moment later, I stood at attention, with my cap in the hand, in front of him.

"What are you going to do now?" he asked.

"Study in Switzerland, Mayor, but first the military service."

"That is not going to happen. You are going to Switzerland. Our country, after that long war, needs youth to study languages and make sure we recover." He loudly exclaimed, "Borreman, the railway-time schedule!" While grumbling and mumbling, he flipped through the little book.

"Ah, here it is—the day after tomorrow at one o'clock from Zwolle. Tomorrow you can pack and say good-bye. Today I will write a letter to the Queen that will say that I exempt you from the military service. Safe trip!"

We were not quite comfortable and hastened to Colonel Suermondt, who we apprised of the decision of the mayor. The Colonel slammed his fist on a table and turned red.

After arriving home, we explained the situation to Father Jan. After a few thoughtful puffs on his cigar, he said, "You should do what the mayor says. In The Hague, they do not dare counter him." And so it transpired.

Maurits Cornelis van Hall, Esq.,
("Papa" and "Opa") 1836 – 1900 ornately dressed.

Herengracht 475, the house of "Opa" van Hall now
the headquarters of the Hollandsche Societeit van Levensverzekeringen.
As a seven year old boy Jan van Hall, the father of the author, once climbed onto
the sundial on top of the façade of the house. Mrs. Barnouw who lived across the
canal noticed this. She immediately sent her house boy, dressed in a pink jacket,
running over the bridge of the Leidsche street to the other side, upon which a
highly upset Mama van Hall was able to guide the young culprit down.

Quite some time later, we received from the Ministry of War an exceptional exemption.

Mayor Van Heemstra ruled as "the first one among his equals" with a firm hand and a heart of gold.

In Hattem lived very old families—Stegeman, Hulsbergen, Van Raalte, and Van der Worp. Several of the families still work their own land or clay quarries, which they had for many centuries, and are from older ancestries than the merchant lineages in Amsterdam.

Almost every morning, the mayor rode in his little carriage through the city and the surrounding areas, the bowlegged Jan van Hattem on the driver's seat, to distribute to the needy and sick citizens food, medicines, and clothes.

The town crier ensured that news was disseminated. How well we still remember when on the thirtieth of April 1909, he announced the birth of a Princess! As fast as we could, we ran home to report the glad tidings.

We lived a distance of a couple of kilometers from the city and factually were outside of the enclosed medieval community. We did attend the wooden-shoe school (*klompenschool*) of Master Van Zuilen.

No child likes to be different from other children. We were better dressed and suffered especially when the mother of the author decided one day that we should wear leather boots. Everyone else wore wooden shoes. It caused us a disadvantage when we were pursued. The boys would take a wooden shoe in each hand and run in their socks. Leather boots could not compete. We experienced that once when we were overtaken and one of the boys with a towering wallop hit us on the head with his wooden shoe, as a result of which it broke in two. The mood of the people changed fast, and we decided to join the group who accompanied the limping boy to his house to witness the whipping that awaited him. Money was scarce for new wooden shoes in Hattem.

It was much worse when we had to wear glasses. Some big boys shoved a little boy to the fore; his flaxen-blond hair covered his forehead, his clear blue eyes, and his ever-present snotty nose. After some stammering, this came out: "Oe-oe, a'k 'n bril zie, moet ik altied poep'n." (*Bril* is Dutch for *glasses* and is also the same word for "toilet seat," so colloquially, he spoke, "When I see glasses/toilet seat, I always have to poop.") There was loud laughter in which we were forced to bittersweetly participate.

In our youth, Hattem did have gas, but no electricity. The mayor explained to us why this was so: "You can smell gas and hear it, and if you hold a match to it, it burns. But if you happen to touch an electrical wire, you don't see anything, and you get a whopper of a punch. That can only be the Devil, and we have enough trouble keeping him outside the gates."

Hattem has its ghosts. *Fladderak* and *Kladdegat* are a kind of hellhound with fiery eyes; they roam at night in the passageways and under the walls. Many a citizen will increase his walk as he passes by those places.

The White Wife (*Witte Wief*) and the White Rabbit (*Wit Kenien*) live in the forest around the castle Molecaten. The legend has it that Mayor Van Heemstra once, on a quiet summer evening, rode through the forest. The evening mist started to form. White wisps floated through the trees and over the Spanish graves, where the casualties of the Spanish war are buried. Suddenly, the mist formed a figure, and Witte Kenien threateningly approached his carriage. "Jan, lay the whip on!" shouted the mayor. With a wild gallop, they proceeded to the city and through the gates to the Church Square. The sparks flew off the cobblestones. The carriage stopped. The mayor spoke to the upset flock of citizens there and warned them that in the future, they should not go to the forest after dark. At that time, we believed the story, but it is more likely that the mayor, in this way, wanted to stop the youth from necking outside the city gates. He had a practical sense of humor!

Once a year, Queen Wilhelmina came to Hattem—not only for Mayor Van Heemstra but really for his sister, the wife of General F. A. Hoefer. In earlier times, she was the governess of the young Wilhelmina. The so-lovely Mrs. Hoefer lived in a big white house that was built on the easterly wall of Hattem. The reader cannot imagine what an event that was. The Queen came to visit us! And then she rode into the little dead end just before the home of the Hoefers. We stood there, the "inside" and "outside" citizens of Hattem, shouting "Long live the Queen!"

The publisher of her book *Lonely but Not Alone*, Mr. Ten Have, was a descendant of the Separatists and came originally from Hattem.

With the cities of Wezep and Wapenfeld, Hattem was a hotbed of the Separatists. How well we remember the quartering of the Dragoons! The mill in Wapenfeld was used for gatherings, and many can tell you how the positions of the blades had to be to indicate that no informers or Dragoons were in the neighborhood to disturb any religious practice.

Echoes of the patriotic times reach us also in Hattem. Our closest neighbors were the Daendels and Van Spengler families. In 1786, the two families fought. The patriot Daendels lived in a big white house just outside of Hattem; it lies in the floodplains on the bank of the river Ijsel and is now a youth hostel. The house of the Orange-minded Captain J. G. van Spengler lay on the west side of the city walls—on the Waa. In September 1786, the States of Holland decided to place a garrison in Hattem because of the independent and once-in-a-while-rebellious attitudes. They sent General J. C. van Spengler, the father of the Captain, with a troop of soldiers forth. Daendels promptly imprisoned the son and let the General know that he would order to have the son and his grandson shot dead if he advanced. The grandson, however, was able, in the middle of the night and while almost naked (he only had a nightshirt flapping behind him and was barefoot), to run through the pastures and forests and reach the castle Molecaten, where General-Major Reinhard Baron van Heeckeren hid him. Perhaps this is the origin of the ghost stories of the Witte Wief and the Wit Kenien. The dauntless General Van Spengler disregarded the ultimatum and gave the order to attack. The resistance was minimal. Only a few cannon shots were fired in the direction of Molecaten and Waarborg. He found his son and grandson unharmed. Luckily, it remained only with the warning.

Daendels escaped to Amsterdam to stand shoulder to shoulder with the young patriot Maurits Cornelis van Hall a year later and take up arms against the Prussians. Incidentally, he did both without much success.

In this "Middle Ages" environment we grew up.

The big event of the year was when we were allowed to visit Amsterdam, where our family really belonged.

In our early youth, we stayed a couple of times with Oma van Hall at the Herengracht 475. We vividly remember how, after playing along the canal, we had to be disinfected. Large white sheets were spread in the children's room, to the left of the entrance under the doorstep. Our mittens, coats, hats, woolen shawls and shoes were then treated with sulfur. We could have contracted tuberolosis outside, from which our great-grandparents died. We, who in Frankhuis and Hattem, in our wooden shoes, were allowed to horse around with our farmer buddies and were continually dirty, until we were put in a lukewarm bath on Saturday evening. In the meantime, bacteria was discovered and milk was particularly dangerous. Therefore female donkeys occasionally were brought to the house on the canal and under the watchful eye of Oma or a servant were milked.[14]

Oma was just as precise with the fish. When the fisherwomen from Zandvoort walked along the Fishermen Trail via restaurant Kraantje Lek in Overveen to Haarlem and catch the train to Amsterdam, then Oma wanted to inspect the fish herself and have a chat with them. Once, a fisherwoman said to her, "May I have a glass of water? I feel kind of weak."

"What is the matter?" asked Oma.

---

[14] The laundry was sent twice a year to the Veluwe because the water in the creek was clear with less danger of bacteria. When the numerous baskets came back, the servants spread the sheets on the floor and treated the baskets and contents with sulfur. Subsequently, the laundry was moved to the laundry room, where the blue sorting tables and presses were, to at last reach the linen closets. In our house, the housewife virtuously does the laundry every Monday.

"Five days ago, I gave birth to a child" came the answer.

In those days, the servants had to eat salmon every day; it was solid food and cheap. Eventually, this became too much and the servants on the canal called a strike with the result that they had to eat salmon only twice a week. Now a serving of smoked salmon costs five guilders in a restaurant. One does not eat this every day anymore!

A couple of years later, after the passing of Oma, we regularly went to Amsterdam and stayed with Aunt Suze van Tienhoven-van Hall and Uncle Aat and Aunt Nel van Hall-Boissevain, the parents of Mayor Gijsbrecht. They lived respectively on the Herengracht 332 and the Keizersgracht 327. The gardens blended together with no fence. A few houses further lived Uncle Walrave Boissevain. What fun we had visiting with our nieces and nephews climbing over the fences of neighbors, who not always were amused. Mayor Gijsbrecht happily participated, although he was obviously breaking the law.

Uncle Aat and Aunt Nel maintained the most welcoming houses one can imagine. In their country home in Hattem, "de Konijnenberg," they spent summer vacations with their ten children. Each child had a large bedroom and could invite a boyfriend or girlfriend. In addition, Aunt Nel always had two girls from Maison de Vries, Amsterdam, who would stay for two weeks and then change places with two other girls from Maison de Vries. Aunt Nel thought they looked pale and needed fresh air. This was long before there were camping grounds and vacation centers.

Our family consisted of eight children, and during the First World War, when it was not possible to travel abroad, we were in Hattem together with over fifty young people. We would go sailing and canoeing, swimming in the river Ijssel and in the family lake, The Kolk, go hiking and bycicling—a carefree youth. The war and the corresponding misery passed us by. Though in 1914, Mrs. De Booy-Boissevain, on behalf of the Amsterdam Comittee, sent around thirty Belgian refugees to Hattem to the address of the mother of this author, soon they felt at home in the quiet and bucolic surroundings, especially the Bacot family from Antwerp, a family of extremely gifted musicians.

• • •

Towards the end of the First World War we visited Grandfather Charles Boissevain.[15]

He had almost a hundred descendants, but when we arrived at "Drafna", the big Norwegian wooden house close to Naarden, we were the only guests and got his undivided attention.

He gave us a book that he had printed, titled *Our Pioneers: The History of Some Members of the Family Boissevain*

"You must read this," he said. "They are the daybooks of your ancestors. During the religious persecutions in France, they escaped to Holland and experienced unbelievably much misery.[16] I hope that my grand- and great-grandchildren will take note of the example of their ancestors because a series of awful wars and revolutions await you. The hundred years of peace and prosperity we have had in our country will soon come to a violent end."

We looked at him with dismay. This did not fit at all in to our pleasant life in Hattem.

"Have you already read *The Socialists* by Quack?" he fired at us while his pince-nez angrily moved up and down on his nose.

"Quack, Quack?" we asked even more upset.

"Yes, my nephew, Prof. H. P. G. Quack. Read that book, and then you will understand what I am talking about."

---

[15]   The wife of Charles Boissevain, Emily McDonnell (Granny), came from Ireland. She descended from Somerled, founder of the "Kingdom of the Isles", who died in battle in 1164 and also from Angus Oge, about whom Sir William Scott composed a poem titled "Ronald, The Lord of the Isles". These islands, amongst which Islay, lie between Scotland and Ireland. The McDonnells were wild gents. Many died in battle but also on their war fleet, which occasionally consisted of over 70 ships. The parents of "Granny", Hercules and Emily Moylan, were married by the blacksmith in Gretna Green. The Moylans from Cork, Ireland, had travelled to London to attend a session of Parliament and present their daughter to London Society. Great was the dismay when one early morning it appeared their daughter had been kidnapped . Accompanied by her chambermaid she had climbed out of her window that night. Admittedly the father of Hercule, Sir Richard, was Provost of Trinity College in Dublin, but the parents had much bigger plans for their daughter. The London "Times" devoted two articles on the abduction because for the first time in history a steam train had been used, preventing the angry father to catch them with his fast horses. After their return the young couple had to get properly married in the St. George, on Hanover Square.

[16]   An ancestor, the Hugeunot Lucas Boissevain, and his family fled to the north in 1686. Hidden in a hay wagon, they crossed the border. One of the dragonders stuck his spear in the hay to see if anyone was hiding there. He wounded the thigh of the mother, but she did not give a peep, and according to family lore, she had the presence of mind to quickly wipe off the blood on the spear. A certain size of the thigh cannot be discounted, as otherwise, the dragonder would have noticed it.

This followed with some rapid French words, which caused us more embarrassment.

"Yes," I said in proper Dutch, "you must strike while the iron is hot."

We realized only later on that the old gentleman did not exaggerate as we earlier thought. Quack's warning, which did not get much attention in his day, we have read. His message stressed that the business owner has to take into account the person and their dignity. During the rapid industrial expansion, the individual seemed simply to have been forgotten. Quack used crass language in his "cry of distress," which can be read in the last part of his work. Grandfather Boissevain, author and journalist understood him. The days of the liberal period were coming to an end. Freedom that does not take into consideration moral values, can lead to injustice and anarchy.

The author had taken the admonition of Mayor Van Heemstra to heart. He learned his languages and also did his best, albeit in a very modest way, to help the country recover. After years of wandering through South America and the Caribbean as an employee of the Royal Dutch Steamship Company he landed shortly before the Second World War in Amsterdam.

There we celebrated our Copper Wedding Anniversary. It was at the end of 1944, the Hunger Winter. We were in the resistance and, together with a group of dockworkers, spent the night without our bride on some hay in a cellar. For this occasion, we had been able to secure a little tobacco and a celebratory bottle. How we talked and talked and then the things they told us—a totally different story from the erstwhile life at the bend of the Herengracht. And a very different wedding celebration.

In the time of Opa Van Hall, the dockworker only got paid when he worked. When during a severe winter or when fog or a storm prevented a ship from coming in, then he starved. Once working, he sometimes worked thirty hours at a time, earning twenty-five cents an hour, no pay when sick or injured on the job, no pension or widow's pension, no vacation, abominable slum dwellings and a miserable existence.

All this is sufficiently well known. However, one aspect in the life of the dockworker struck us as particularly immoral.

When a dockworker wanted to work, he had to go to his pub and wait till the pub keeper got a message from a shipowner or shipping agent that a vessel needed to take on cargo or drop cargo off. In the meantime, the pub keeper abundantly served his group jenever and put it on their tab. The workers who had drunk the most were the first to be sent to the boat. Then in row boats came the so-called keg men, "*kistjesmannen*," to serve them, an extra tot while working. In this manner, they got used to drinking alcohol. And then, mind you, the shipowner would pay the wages not to the dockworker, but to the pub keeper, who would then deduct their bar tab.

In those days, charitable organizations would hang up signs next to the pubs on which a pale woman holding a small child and surrounded by other children would call out, "Oh, Father, oh, no more"—"*Ach, Vader, ach, niet meer.*" Mischievious pranksters would then write after "Ach" a "t" (in Dutch, "Acht" is eight) so that one now would read, "Eight, Father, eight, not more."[17]

Father did not really want to drink, however when he didn't, he had less chance for a job. The Stevedore's Act in 1916 put a stop to this corrupt system. Since then, alcohol has disappeared from the harbor. When one now sees a drunk, it is most likely a foreign sailor.

In our discussions with the dockworkers, we noticed that the remembrances of these abusive situations was very much alive. The distrust of the employer is still large, although the working conditions have radically improved.

We once asked Henk Gortzak, a former foreman of the Communist Party in Amsterdam, how he became a communist. His answer: "My father was a dockworker." Case closed, period.

Luckily, not every laborer's child who experienced the social abuses in the Amsterdam Harbor or the general nineteenth-century work conditions turned to the same doctrine of the Communist Party. Take for example Suurhoff, the former Minister of Social Welfare and Public Health. His grandfather, a descendant of a well-to-do Friesian farm family, found work in the Amsterdam Harbor and became a victim of the widespread abuse of alcohol. The stories of the sorrowful youth of his mother made an indelible impression on the young Suurhoff and, together with the always-present worries about old age in the household, became one of the main impulses for the work he later did to change the social conditions.

The "always too little and always too late" of the liberal period generated strong reactions. The pendulum of the clock swings then much further. Perhaps that is the reason why, over the last years, there has been a movement toward governmental control and central planning. The state has become the biggest capitalist. The private individual is now a shareholder in the corporation, anonymous and powerless. The contrast between capital and labor has blurred. This has resulted in how the employer and employee relate; in increasing degree, they conduct themselves as equal partners.

The pendulum of the clock will have to swing a lot more before it can find a more harmonic rhythm. Standing still is not possible.

---

[17]   Another version was "Respect Father no more"—"Acht Vader niet meer."

Unnoticed, we have landed in the hot topics of today and have far surpassed the intent of our little book. Therefore, we return to the son of Opa, Uncle Aat.

But not before we report on a statement by Karl Marx as it appeared over a century ago, on 31 December 1853, in the *Tribune* in New York:

"The people of the West will rise again to power and unity of purpose, while the Russian Colussuss itself will be shattered by the progress of the masses and the explosive force of ideas."

These words of Karl Marx have not been included in his collected works—definitely not in Russia.

Uncle Aat, eighty-seven years old, is still alive. He is the head of the Van Hall family. He is a banker with clear-headed intellect and a heart of gold. He has taken on the care of hundreds of family members, including those furthest removed. Together with Aunt Nel, he advises and supports them in their troubles. Even many who are not related to him, have also visited him—never in vain.

The tradition of the family forbids us to describe him while he is alive. That can only happen later.

We will make an exception for the Van Kinsbergen Foundation, of which he has been the chairman for years. The reason for this is that it brings us back to 1795 and the old Maurits Cornelis. Actually, it is not really a foundation. In 1819, Admiral Van Kinsbergen passed away, and in his will, a part of his fortune was set aside to annually support a number of institutions. Five trustees have the task to manage the fortune. The first appointed were Maurits Cornelis and, among others, his friends J. Sinderam and D. Hooft. Since then, a Van Hall has always been part of the board of the directors. Following the old Maurits were his son Floris Adriaan, son Frederik, Opa Van Hall, Uncle Aat, and lastly Mayor Gijsbert.

Together with the "Schipluydenfonds"—the Crewmember Trust—of the municipality of Elburg, an elementary school is operated there.

Per the instructions of the will, the five board members must meet once a year in the "best hotel" in the country and partake of a festive banquet. The bust of the admiral is placed on the table, and the chairman must hold a laudatory speech. To broaden the awareness of the speech, each year a number of guests are invited. Already, a hundred and forty times has the praise been sung, and the trustees endeavor themselves each time to find something new.[18]

So at last, we have landed with Gijsbrecht.

We will have to limit ourselves to a report of some personal details. Just like Oom Aat, we cannot give a description of his life. Although he is not the head of the family who needs to be treated with deference, as mayor, he is the head of the police with whom we, up to now, have a reasonable relationship. So far, we have only one fine.

Gijsbrecht studied law in Leiden. He became a banker, initially in New York and then in Amsterdam. His career includes many positions in the societal and social fields.

He married Emmie Nijhoff. She studied history in Amsterdam.

It is a relief to write about another family and devote a few words to the Nijhoff family.

Emmie van Hall–Nijhoff belongs to the eleventh generation of Nijhoffs, who came in 1637 from Weseke (Westfalen) to Arnhem. The paths of the ancestors of Gijs and Emmie have crossed many times since that time. This must have started in Arnhem, as the city did not have more than six thousand inhabitants. The Van Halls lived initially on the otherside of the Rhine in Malburgen and then later a few kilometers outside Arnhem in Klingenbeek. They naturally came regularly to the "big city." Thus, Allert Florisz van Hall, on 24 March 1660, made public in Arnhem the announcement of the intended marriage to Naletien Teunissen.

The Nijhoffs were clerks for the city secretaries. We read how Isaac Nijhoff received fifty guilders in 1728 for transferring the city's archive to a new location. This archive had been unceremoniously dumped seven years before above the secretariat. Fifty guilders was not insignificant, but probably this task generated much more profit later on. Perhaps the sifting through the archives aroused his love of books and writings. Jacob Nijhoff, the son of Isaac, became the first of six generations of booksellers, publishers, and printers.

---

[18] The "Dickens Fellowship" has taken on a similar task. It was established well over a half a century ago in London. Many branches were established across the world, also in our country in Haarlem and Zwolle. Each year a conference takes place where a prominent person gives a laudatory speech about "the immortal memory" of Dickens. In 1958, in England, this honor fell to Dutch author Godfried Bomans. On 7 February, the birthday of Dickens, a laudatory speech is given. At the moment, a hundred and fourteen speeches have been held and Dickens is fast catching up with Van Klinsbergen. The score is now Van Klinsbergen, 140, and Dickens, 114.

In 1834, Maurits Cornelis van Hall, Esq., in his role as the expert legal adviser of the members of The Association Furthering the Interest of the Booktrade (established 1817), presented to the King a preliminary draft of a law covering the book trade. They were struggling because there was no copyright law. This association has counted among its board a number of Nijhoffs, including Emmie's father and grandfather (honorary members).

Via the Dutch author Multatuli, both families stayed in contact. Multatuli was, as it happens, very friendly with one of his publishers, G. L. Funke, co-founder and director of the newspaper *Nieuws van den Dag*, and grandfather on the mother's side of Emmie.

The Nijhoffs have produced publishers, writers, and poets and accomplished much in the scientific field. The poet M. Nijhoff was Emmie's nephew. Her brother Wouter is the President-Director of Martinus Nijhoff's Booktrade & Publishing Company.

In the area of the stage, a relationship between the families could have existed, as J. N. van Hall, Esq., was the founder of the Academy of the Performing Arts. If only Emmie's sister, Loudi, the well-known Dutch actress, had not studied acting abroad.

WALRAVEN VAN HALL, 1906–1945

It is not possible to write about Gijs without immediately thinking about his younger brother Walraven, who gave his life for the resistance.

Wally attended the maritime academy in Terschelling and sailed for a number of years as a first mate in the merchant marine. When the war started, he was a banker in Zaandam.

He was a man vibrant with life and energy. If we have to give a description of him, we will cite without hesitation "fighter against injustice" as his most remarkable trait. In battle, he could be hard, but he was also hard on himself.

After the war, a number of members of the resistance wrote letters to the parents of Wally in which they recounted their interactions with him. Below we give a little anthology. It is not possible to give a complete report. The facts are missing. During the years of the occupation, the maxim applied that one was allowed to know as little as possible about the activities of the other resistance members. Almost everybody worked under a pseudonym, and it was forbidden to ask, even under misplaced curiosity, a real name. When the Gestapo applied the rack, one could not, after all, betray information one did not know. And so many brave souls died taking their secrets into their graves.

The letters were bundled and appeared in print. We tried to place, to some degree, the snippets in chronological order.

It was in the Fall of 1941 when my friend De Visser asked me after a clandestine meeting, if I would be interested in trying to organize aid for the seafaring families. The work for this was started, on the initiative of Capt. Filippo from Hilligersberg in Rotterdam and surrounding areas, and because Amsterdam harbored a large number of these families, it was highly necessary that attention be paid to these families. This was during the time when the occupier had decided that the families of those who were sailing for the Allies could not receive an allowance of more than ninety guilders (aside from the small child benefit). Shortly after I took the first steps, De Visser asked me on a certain morning (the date is not known; we did not write anything down) to join him at the Krasnapolsky Hotel to make the acquaintance of a certain Van Hall. After we met a meeting was planned in Hilligersberg. Together with Wally we made the voyage to Rotterdam by train and tram to Hilligersberg.

In the beginning of 1942 a ship owner from Rotterdam came to my office, with whom I had a business relationship, and told me that in Rotterdam a principal committee was formed for the aid of seafarer families; to this end a few persons in Rotterdam had gathered a hundred fifty thousand guilders; and why, he said, could not Amsterdam do the same? He mentioned the name of Meerveld, who dealt with this and who he would bring along that afternoon. In the afternoon he returned and I found him with Wally, who was delighted with my surprise when I discovered who this "Meerveld" was. The three of us discussed a plan to coordinate the activities of all the committees involved with seafarers, to be able to develop a united front and to work more effectively.

On a sunny, cold winter morning, end of January 1943, a few people came together from different parts of the country and different sections of our Dutch Society; they were a representative of Prof. Heringa (Nieuwenhuizen), v.d. Bosch (v.d. Berg), originally from Eindhoven but in hiding in Groningen, Van Hall (Van Tuyl), Jos. v. Hövell tot Westerflier (v. Veen), Deni Mesritz (Mulder) and Valkenburg. In a very special method we were brought together on the Leidschegracht, some had a distinguishing mark with them, others a coin with a special cross, or a word with a particular meaning. We represented groups of persons, who had definite principles in that the German needed to be fought on the basis of spiritual resistance. Prof. Heringa was at that time busy harnessing the civil servants, Van Hall was already working on the finances, principally for the benefit of the seafarers, v.d. Bosch had run into espionage difficulties at

Philips and was preparing in the northern part of our country the National Relief Fund action—*N.S.F.*—still very modest in size then, while the foundations were being laid for the National Committee—*N. C.*

It was a sunny morning and in the quiet room in the back of Wally's mother's house the foundation for a closely knit cooperation was established, which remained, and over the years was broadened and deepened. None of them are alive, they were killed directly or indirectly by the German, except Valkenburg, who thus can confirm it.

With his intense eyes and his barely controlled urgency to forge together a so necessary united front to become one, of understanding, of doing, and for responsibility, Van Hall sat in the middle of that circle, and listened and called himself "only an observer," because it involved an approach between what Prof. Heringa was preparing and what the National Committee wanted. The conversation incidentally proceeded smoothly, the will to work together was present, and Wally continually helped us through details and kept track of the main purpose. He did not make an easy impression, he was already then not a man who could be satisfied with loose comments and consistently highlighted the consequences of agreements and the necessity to convert this or that act into specifics.

After a stay of six months in Scheveningen, I luckily was released and came on 4 November 1942 back home. Right after my arrival home Wally was there as one of the first to shake my hand and I still see him standing in front of my door, carrying a huge basket of fruit.

Around two months later I was back on my feet, partly due to a two week stay in Sinderen at the initiative of Wally; he came over to talk and together we agreed that I could slowly go back to work. Through this work, establishing different contacts in Amsterdam, the National Relief Fund was able to grow. Initially we impatiently wanted to start helping the people in hiding, though we agreed that we needed much money for that. In the summer of 1943 Wally showed up one morning with the announcement: "Better start now, 80,000 guilders are ready to be spent."

In August 1943 I had a long conversation with him about the need for financial support for the persecuted Jews. According to me something had to happen soon and on a large scale. Only Van Hall in my thinking could help. However he did not want to participate as he was afraid that all his other work would be endangered. I tried to convince him otherwise, but although he recognized the need and the duty of the Dutch people to address this, he continued to refuse. This is the only time that I disappointedly left him. Shortly thereafter however, I noticed that a large scale support for the Jews was organized and soon it became apparent that also in this, Wally was the man.

Wherever the big machine of the movement threatened to seize up, Wally popped up and as he so characteristically said he had to function as the oiler. Without agreeing in advance, everyone naturally accepted he was the person in charge. The so-called "Delta," the precursor of the future Internal Forces—B.S. [Binnenlandse Strijdkrachten]—was organized by him, and the railroad strike could get financed through his efforts.

When we had to escape from Zaandam and found a place in Amsterdam, we sat every evening together and the first thing we always talked about was Westzijde 42. Often he would say, "Brinkie, that is my only fear, that I would have to leave my family behind if something happens." Indeed this was his only fear, because in other areas he was not frightened by anything or anybody. Without ever placing himself in the fore ground, he was able to take hold of the most dangerous situations. I can't recite all the cases, but one I briefly want to mention. When Elizabeth Boissevain was arrested she had the key with her of Delta C., the Head Quarters of the Commander of the Internal Forces [Binnenlandse Strijdkrachten] General Koot. Since a lot of compromising material was there, our names and many weapons, we had a meeting that evening joined by a third person. We could not establish contact with one of our armed crews, but before the S.D. [Siecherheist Dienst] came, we had to empty out the place. "Then we have to do it ourselves," he said and we went at 5:30 in the morning, in the dark, to Keizersgracht 533. Although we grumbled, we had to wait outside and he sneaked alone and unarmed into the house knowing that the S.D. could be sitting there. Thank God Lies (*Elizabeth*) kept silent and we could undisturbed and quickly empty out the office. Looking backward many people will say: so much courage is not really needed, but in my eyes it was extremely courageous. In this manner we had tens of cases like this about which not a word was spoken and did not become known. That was the real Wally van Hall, he was a quiet hero.

Putting aside his own being he was always ready to do very dangerous jobs himself. It was always: "Brinkie, tomorrow I have again some dangerous fireworks, don't you think it is better if I do it myself?" or "Hey, tomorrow some English pilots need to be picked up and brought away, shall I do it?"

In May 1943 my wife and I belonged to the participants of the attack on the Labor Exchange [*Gew. Arbeidsbeurs*] in Zaandam. Through a coincidence of circumstances we ended up in danger due to one of the accomplices. On the advice of Mr. Soepboer, Chief of Police in Hemburg, a fellow accomplice, I established contact with Walraven. It was a very delicate matter and I considered him extremely capable to clear things up, which he promptly did with the assistance of Mr. Buys. From that day I came more often into contact with him. Among other things delivering paper for newspapers, printing of various articles, etc. He also promptly introduced me to Gerrit van der Veen and his niece Suzan van Hall.

January 1944. Snow and raids in the Netherlands. In the evening at 6 o'clock received a letter from the Haarlem District Head with the instruction to deliver this that evening to a certain address in Zaandam. We have to make haste as Zaandam is being punished and everyone has to be inside by 8 o'clock. A kraut had been assaulted. Arriving at the correct address my ringing the bell is answered by the opening of a hatch in the door. After my message "coming from K in Haarlem," quiet consultations were held, after which I was led inside. A large room, a bright fire in the fire place, in front of which two men and the lady of the house. The courier is invited to join the circle and while the letter is quickly read, I look around and see on the mantelpiece a portrait of an old gentleman with a beard, who I recognize as a personal friend of my father. Wally discusses the letter with the fourth person in the room and throws it into the fireplace. Then I receive instructions and now I already notice how fast Wally works with both his head and hands. Quickly I am sent out the door as the clock of obedience is ticking away.

Every illegal worker knows and still thinks back with some fright, how he can count with almost mathematical certainty on new, sometimes breathtaking problems.

Was there not always something dreadful? It started with the seemingly simple declaration of being Aryan or not. Then the arrests of the Jews followed, slowly, but wretchedly certain, to include ultimately the sick and the very aged.

Oh, the arrests of those helpless old people! The problem of shelter, later the problem of maintenance. First the provision of food permits, later the provision of food and the food permits, thousands of issues, the threats of arrests of the hosts, the military and working men, later the frightful house to house street raids, the making of hiding places in feverish haste. Identity cards, inserts, later registration cards and new stamps and the suspenseful time during the process, the guesses, and thinking if you were going to succeed or not. The anxiety of all those people who were dependant on us. And finally the ID cards [*Ausweise*] and especially at the border areas, the constantly changing orders to move [*marsch-befehle*] and condemnations.

And then the bombardments, the homeless, the forced moving in together, the quartering of German soldiers and the concealed residents.

Was it a wonder that one of our colleagues time and again remarked: "Fright upon fright, how does a person stay healthy?"

What could we have started, if there were not a few, those pillars, who oversaw the total secret movement and kept it in control?

Often we had a religious conversation; and then with a certain pride Wally frequently mentioned that he always was a Calvinist and that he was always attracted to it, though through circumstances his life took a different path from the liberal way. He was aware of the religious conditions in our country and he liked to discuss it.

In Wally hid the eternal naughty boy and I would like to give one example:

We were invited (before the War) to an engagement party. It turned out to be a minimally fun party: lemonade and no smoking. In the middle of the party Wally whispered to me: "If you want wine, then come with me."
He brought me to the dumb waiter and called with a fake ladies voice: "Jan—two wines." Jan answered: "Yes Madam" and two glasses of wine arrived from downstairs. Wally had discovered that the Lady of the house served wine to some of the older guests and got it herself from the dumb waiter.
We continued the game till Jan answered: "The bottle is empty, Ma'am."

What stays most with me are his eyes, often tired, but trustworthy, and with a wonderful luminosity of a benevolent and persevering man, who knows he is called upon. And then his hands. When he sat quietly with me, in a seeming impasse, but ready to make an elegant gesture accompanying his words, as for example: "but I have to do the support work in Leeuwarden, nobody else will do it."

And then always: his almost French disposition, his "esprit," with witty remarks describing a situation, giving himself too small a role, as if he is not important.

The staircase, Herengracht 475

Walraven van Hall, 1906 - 1945

On Mondays he came to the stock exchange at the Commodity Exchange. A quick raising of the head, and along different routes we found ourselves in an agreed upon quiet corner.

A few comments on his work, a spirited discussion and the "elusive pimpernel" disappeared in the crowd.

During my visit to London in Oct/Nov 1944 it became evident in a number of conversations with Her Royal Highness, our Queen, that she knew of him and valued his contributions.

In the first days of September 1944 it turned out that the archives of the Relief Fund disappeared, in which the application forms of numerous relief cases were housed, including the suitcases which held them.

For everyone involved this was life threatening when a blackmail letter was received in which threats were made to turn over to the Sicherheitsdienst the pertinent documents. Then "Van Tuyl" got involved and I invited him once to my house. He did not need to announce his name to me and my wife—the resemblance with his father was immediately noticeable to us.

I remember the discussion we had over this precarious subject, his vehement indignation and the fierceness of his reaction. With his involvement it was possible to retrieve the documents from the hands of the thief without any mishaps. He was the man who had the relationships with the hit squads, who occupied themselves with this type of work, and once we arrived at this point we knew who was responsible for the theft.

May 1943 brought forth the problem of people in hiding to escape imprisonment and the around that time already fired civil servants or in hiding because of their refusal to serve, professors with anti-German positions, theater actors against the required German cultural criteria, all needing support, which became the foundation for the National Support Fund [*Nationaal Steunfonds*].

In the meantime assurance was received from London that money lent for active resistance was guaranteed by the government, as a result of which we could complete loans, which occurred on a large scale. Many times we discussed the difficulties with these loans, with the biggest obstacle faced by the large moneylenders, the banks, who could not record in their books "Loan to the National Support Fund" or something like that, but had to create a not very transparent entry, that would be plausible to the not always trustworthy bank employees.

Wally liked to pose a like problem and the next time would come up with a most ingenious solution.

Along with all the financial support, other organizations were formed such as the Country Wide Persons in Hiding Organization [*Landelijke Onderduikers-organizatie*] which dealt with the placement of Persons in Hiding, the old Regulatory Service [*Orde Dienst*] already formed in 1940 by the army and represented the first kernels of active resistance, all of which needed more coordination. Here Wally started his major work, first the finances and later taking the lead of all these groups.

A group that presented special financial difficulties were the Jews in Hiding; for them loans were not available, and we couldn't count on them for active resistance. Because I was in contact with a few groups, we could form to this end a completely separate committee, where initially Gotzen and Aten, I believe he called himself Schuurman or something like that, would work totally independent and outside the support groups. Due to the apprehension of Gotzen, he was quickly replaced. For this we needed to collect more cash, which I did with F. de Boer.

In the meantime the system was continually being perfected. Gijs can tell you about this, how he controlled the central cash, notes of remittance were signed and especially by Wally large sums were lent. Wally would then lightheartedly talk about how he travelled from the East, the province Twente, with a million guilders, as if talking about having bought a cigar.

When complications arose between Gijs and the people coming to collect the money, I offered my office as a safe haven and since then the notes of remittance were brought to my office and money paid out against them, which ultimately amounted to about eighty million guilders. Through my contact with the Regulatory Service [*Orde Dienst*] I mediated several times meetings, such as a radio operator who was caught out in Zaandam and hidden by the Regulatory Service, groups in the Regulatory Service who were in danger, raids on distribution centers who needed help etc.

By working with all the groups, Wally became more and more the central figure and was involved in ever increasing activities, furthered by his charming manner and sharp intellect that attracted many people.

After the September Days of 1944 Wally was Minister-President of everything concerning the resistance; financially everything was brought into the National Support Fund [*Nationaal Steunfonds*] and by forming the illegal committee of the Countrywide Organization [*Landelijke Organizatie*] the National Support Fund, Trouw, the Netherlands Domestic Armed Forces [*Nederlandse Binnenlandse Strijdkrachten*] one central place came into existence, where all resistance efforts could be managed.

Because I was principally involved with the Netherlands Domestic Armed Forces [*Nederlandse Binnenlandse Strijdkrachten*] from that time on I had little to do with the National Support Fund [*Nationaal Steunfonds*]. I still saw Wally, once or every other week, when he came for the lunch at my office, where I was every Wednesday; then he talked about typical human problems, questions about the sense of honor, plans for the future, the Foundation 1940–1945 etc.

On 27 January 1945 the whole assembly of the Country Wide Work Committee [*Landelijk Werk Comité*] which was sadly attended by almost everybody, was captured by the Grüne Polizei and everyone was transported to the prison on the Weteringschans. On 12 February Wally and a few others were executed by a firing squad. What ever happened in those intervening days we will never hear about, but the fact that no searches of houses or arrests of colleagues occurred, proved the absolute silence of Wally and his fellow prisoners.

And then I came on 13 February to our address Leidsegracht 48.

Mrs. Koppenal, paler than usual, asked me "Do you already know about Mr. van Tuyl?" (Wally).

"No Ma'am, what is the matter?"

"They killed him yesterday in Haarlem."

"The rats."

Then I ran away so fast, because I did not want to show my tears. Shortly after the liberation, as a member of the Purification Committee, I had to sentence traitors in the prison on the Weteringschans. We had to go into the prison. In a corner cell, the last in a row, among many names scratched into the wall, was "W. VAN HALL."

I can still write those letters, slightly curved upward, to this day.

Thus here Wally fought his last heavy battle. Here he struggled with all the problems around those he loved most on earth. But the letters are firm and without hesitation scratched in to the wall.

Poor van Tuyl?

No, strong Walraven van Hall.

After his completed battles and after offering the highest price, still yet: the fortunate Walraven van Hall.

The Netherlands owes him great gratitude.[19]

His friends saw him this way.

The letters were written shortly after his death and the liberation; they were very emotional days. But fourteen years later since the war, his thinking and action had taken more defined shapes; Wally's stature has grown larger in our eyes.

Inadvertently, our thoughts went back to Great-Grandfather Anne Maurits, the fighter against injustice and for religion. And then they went back to his brother Floris Adriaan, the minister. But what a difference there is in their relationships as brothers to life.

---

[19]   Just like every year, thousands of people went on 4 May 1959 to the Honorary Graveyard in the dunes near Overveen to commemorate the fallen. Under the chimes of the bells, the people slowly made their way to the big cross, which is visible for miles in the rays of the setting sun. After arriving at the top, we saw not far from the entrance a tombstone with "Walraven van Hall, 1909–1945." A little farther, we saw the names of two young brothers: Jan Karel Boissevain (1920–1943) and Gideon Willem Boissevain (1921–1943). There we saw also the name of their cousin Louis Daniel Boissevain (1922–1943). All three were executed on the same day. A remarkable number of young people who did not experience the war had come that evening. Almost all had brought some flowers. Attentively they looked at the plaque close to the bell tower; in bronze letters, it describes why the fallen fought and the reasons why they offered their young lives. At eight o'clock, the bells fell silent. On top of the dunes stands, as a silhouette against the golden sky, a trumpeter. The last taps were played.

Minister Floris did support Anne Maurits financially and helped him with housing, but he distanced himself from the proceedings against the dissenters and the transition to the Reformed religion.

Gijsbert stood shoulder to shoulder with Wally.

"Wally hoped that after the liberation the political life in the Netherlands would be freed from the previously narrow minded personal or group interests and that a larger cooperation for the betterment of the Dutch people could be pursued," we read in one of the letters. On that his thoughts for the future were directed.

The suffering during the war and the urge to help each other and to become involved in the resistance against the Germans slowly forged the Dutch people together. Columns, political and religious differences, disappeared. One was ready to share with others the little they had and put their life at risk to organize help or participate in active resistance.

They were horrible years but perhaps the best ones of our life due to the feeling of solidarity, the willingness to sacrifice, and the love of one's fellow man that arose from them.

And then the emotions of the liberation that Wally could not experience came.

We were totally exhausted shortly before the big day. It had become too much. Our work brought us to Amsterdam, and we regularly came into contact with the starving, emaciated people who walked along the harbors, hoping to find some food on board the rare local ships that still came to Amsterdam from the north or the east. The children presented a heartrending sight. They shuffled along on little legs that were as thin as matchsticks, once in a while with bare feet, numb with cold, and with not-understanding big eyes.

We made our way on a bicycle with wooden tires from Amsterdam to the sickbed in our house in Bentveld. We had heard through the radio that the Allied airplanes would drop packets of food. The next morning, they appeared above our house with thundering motors. We dragged ourselves to the window and looked; the packets fell to the right and to the left.

It was an overwhelming spectacle. Once in a while, a packet burst open. On the flat roof of our house, an American flag was spread out; one of the airplanes dove down and flipped his wings. It would take days before the food could be distributed, though it seemed as if the hunger was diminishing. Some villains kept the packets to themselves. How did we punish them? Each was placed on an old scaffold with a sign that said, "Thief of food of his fellow man!"

The liberation brought forth an incident. We had lost a sense of reality and also, for the first time in our life, a sense of humor.

Before his departure from Amsterdam, the Consul of the United States had entrusted us with the consular flag with the request that we would fly it on the day of liberation. Proudly the flag was waving when we heard angry German voices outside from our sickbed. We saw an angry, one-eyed SS general who wanted his sergeant to lower the flag. The wife of the author bravely defended her cloth.

"Where did you get the idea to raise that flag?" asked the general.

"I am an American," she answered. "This is *my* flag, and the war is over."

"If I had known this earlier, then I would have imprisoned you a long time ago. And for *me*, the war is not over."

Totally overwrought, we went to find guns so we could shoot the general and his helper. Luckily for us, the weapons were so well hidden that it took us a while to find them. Sometime later, we looked out the window and saw the Germans had disappeared. The flag was torn to pieces and burned.

Agitatedly we went to the recently arrived Canadian general, Foster. He was quartered a few houses away. It was remarkable how the Canadians, in comparison with the Dutch, looked so healthy and well cared for.

We submitted our protest but received only the answer that from a judicial point of view, the case was not simple as from the German point of view, they had not capitulated to the Americans. He said a lawyer would research it and asked if we could return the next day.

When the second conversation took place, we were somewhat calmer—in part due to the precious pack of cigarettes they had given us earlier.

"The situation is actually very simple," said General Foster. "I have eight hundred men and a handful of tanks. Your SS general has thirty thousand well-rested soldiers and heavy weapons. It is known to me that he does not recognize the capitulation. I am deathly afraid of an incident. Then we will be wiped out. So please forget about the flag. In the meantime, the USA can be proud of your wife," he finished with a twinkle in his eye.

THE DISASTROUS STORM OF 1953

It appears that only a national catastrophe can unite the Dutch people. This unity existed also after the disastrous storm of 1953.

It was, during the Second World War, a veritable experience to see how differences in class and the silos ceased. After the war, the bickering started up again, and the silos were carefully being built once more.

The horrible storm of 1953 brought us all together again for a moment, and no sacrifice was too big. And the sacrifices came not only from our countrymen. Our allies from the Second World War rushed to our aid; our former enemies, the Germans and the Italians, helped too. It was an uplifting scene to see our former opponents helping out in Zeeland.

Through a coincidence, the author experienced the rescue operation up close.

The reader must clearly understand that he did not play a heroic part in the relief effort in Zeeland. He happened to own a small boat that was much needed, and found the resources to richly supply the boat with blankets and food. It was thanks to the skipper Willem de Vreugd, a man from Katwijk, and young fishermen from Oudedorp that the flat-bottomed motorboat, the *Spitfire*, could contribute in a small way to the large relief action. They were men who belonged to the best section of the population of the Netherlands and men in whose outlook on life was written the words "faith and love of one's fellow man."

And although our forefathers have already told us what lay in their hearts, we want to conclude their story with a few annotations we made at that time.

The *Spitfire* was an open and flat-bottomed oak motorboat; it was seven and a half meters long and with a depth of barely fifty centimeters. A canvas spray hood provided protection against everything wet.

On Saturday evening, 31 January 1953, the night of the disastrous storm, we had gathered with many friends and family members to hear a lecture in the house of a cousin, Tom de Booy, whose son Tom Jr., together with Dr. Egelen, had climbed the mountain peaks of the Andes in South America on a geological expedition. That evening, we would hear their story, which was accompanied with slides. The captivating story, which we breathlessly listened to, was disturbed, however. It was already storming when we arrived, but now wind blasts blew through the chimney of the big open fireplace so fiercely that once in a while, the speaker could not be understood. The storm then made the house shake fearfully. Occasionally, the phone would rattle with alarming reports from the life-saving stations. We also were called to the phone. "Pappie, the chimney has been blown away from the roof." "Just let it lie there," we advised, "and go to bed."

At that time, none of us realized the magnitude of the catastrophe that was taking place. We still did not realize it the following morning. In Zandvoort, we saw how frighteningly high the sea was, the low tide notwithstanding; it rolled against the dunes and washed over the boulevard. In Ijmuiden, some ships were lifted up and thrown onto the quay or the street. No personal injuries had occurred, and according to the master of the sea locks, not for one moment were the locks in danger. Only in the course of Sunday evening did the realization that not only Rotterdam and the islands in the south were hit, sink in but in the isolated Zeeland, there was a true disaster.

Our flat-bottomed motorboat was strong and seaworthy but of no value if the captain was a dilettante. Thus the first concern was the finding of an experienced mariner, and who could we better ask for than Willem de Vreugd, the retired captain of the HKS *De Hoop* (the hospital-church ship serving the fishermen) who had sailed on the North Sea for almost half a century and had fished along the coast for a number of years in a flat-bottomed motorboat?

On Tuesday, 3 September, in the early morning, the flat-bottomed motorboat *Spitfire* left Rotterdam with Moerdijk as its destination; it left with Skipper De Vreugd, Deckhand Leibbrand, and me. The boat was loaded with blankets, hundreds of cans of orange juice and milk, all kinds of food, jenever, coffee, and cartons of cigarettes.

In Moerdijk, we heard that very bad news was just received from Schouwen-Duiveland and that we had to go to Bruinisse.

On the Hollandsch Diep (a wide river and estuary of the Rhine and Meuse Rivers) steamed a mighty armada heading to the southwest. There were inland water vessels and fishing boats from everywhere and small navy boats. Then we saw the English, the Americans, the Germans, the Belgians, and even the Swiss coming down the Rhine. All were going to the southwest.

Our radio was continuously on. The cries for help were not meaningless.

"The mayor of Oostland urgently requests small boats. If they do not come soon, the consequences will be horrific."

"The mayor of Nieuwerkerk requests flat-bottomed boats to fetch people from the farms."

And so it went on. Now we knew what to do because in the armada, there were very few small boats like the *Spitfire*.

The motor ran on full power. We carved through every sandbank and used every current that could give us an advantage.

On the easterly dike of Overflakkee, silhouetted against the last sunbeams of the setting sun, a small boy carefully led the way for a group of people. Behind him were two men with a stretcher on their shoulders; then we saw a woman with a child in her arms. Slowly, almost solemnly, they walked to an assistance vessel that lay a distance farther against the dike. Behind the dike was only water, and only then did I realize that all that water was salt water.

After arriving in Bruinisse, we saw that all the houses were underwater. In the street were a couple of drowned cars. There were a few men in rubber boots dredging. Here and there were kerosene lamps. "Where is the mayor?" I asked. A policeman arrived. "How do we get into the polder?" I asked. "Not from here. Just steam along the dike to the northwest, toward the North Sea. There are breaches enough.[20] In Sirjansland, there should be sixty people sitting in the church," he said.

Quickly we were on our way. We sailed in the darkness. Lighthouses and concrete fortifications did not have lights anymore. Our battery did not work anymore. We also did not have any lights. Our spotlight was useless.

Suddenly, in front of us materialized the bow of a tugboat. Both vessels went backward. "Do you see those two small lights?" said the skipper of the tugboat. "That is a small shrimper anchored next to a state water boat. They exactly know the situation."

"It is the *Ouddorp 5*," said Skipper Van Noord. (Ouddorp, on the opposite side, was also underwater.) The other boat was *De Kil*, and it also had a skipper named Van Noord. They were brothers.

During the day, their crew, in three rowboats, sailed into the polder through the big breach in the dike between Sirjansland and Dreischor. They had not returned. "Then we will go after them" was our first reaction. "Certainly not," said the Van Noord brothers. "Your boat will, with the fast current, smash into a wall or whatever, and you will not be able to go on."

In the evening, an old, heavily loaded rowboat approached through the dike. There were ten people on board—an old man, women and children, and

---

[20] Afterward, it turned out that there were more than fifty breaches.

two babies. They found shelter in the cabin of *De Kil*. Our friends had practically no supplies, thus the *Spitfire* offered 10 to 15 blankets, their first warm meal, chocolates, cigarettes, and cans of orange juice and milk. With a marlinespike, we made two holes in each of the cans, which were ready for use and had no danger of contamination. One suffered of thirst in Zeeland in those days.

"What now?" I asked the fishermen.

"Early tomorrow morning, we go with you and your boat" was the answer.

De Kil had a small but excellent transmitter on board and a competent radio operator. "I am the only connection with the outside world," he said, "and I also pass on the messages of amateurs to Hilversum [the location of the National Radio]. How did you actually find yourselves here?"

"Through the radio messages," I answered.

"Ha, I sent those messages to Oosterland and so on, but I don't have an extra receiver to hear if Hilversum correctly passes them on. May I have the unit from the *Spitfire*?"

Then it rained with nightly messages: "Urgently need . . .," "Flat-bottomed boats . . .," "Make light . . .," "Marketplace Middelburg . . .," "Airplane is looking for you . . .," "Rubber boots . . .," "Boats . . .," "Boats . . .," and "Boats . . ."

The sea, pushed by the high tide, streamed that night as a turbulent waterfall through the breach in the dike. The moon shone on a white frozen *Spitfire*. We departed. The young fishermen from Ouddorp, S. van der Klooster and Jan Kastelein, showed us the way.

The polder—it was not to be believed; it was once normal land. We sailed past collapsed farmhouses, barns, chicken coops, underwater standing hedges, poles, gates, telephone wires, barbed wires, and electrical wires—all were so dangerous for the propeller. Dirty brown water moved in unreasonable and unpredictable directions. It was a Sargasso Sea of hay, straw, carcasses, broken household effects, and driftwood. There was an ominous silence. No light or life was to be found.

The daybreak began. Then we saw in the half dark a church, a windmill, and a number of houses around them. Carefully the *Spitfire* approached. There was no sign of life. We blew on the ship's horn. There was no movement, no light, no white flags—we arrived too late; it was three days after the storm.

"There! There! A light!" shouted one of the young fishermen. "On the other side of the village! Quick!"

It was the navigation light of the *Ierseke 15*, a mussel boat. We saw a second boat. How courageous they were to come here with vessels fifteen meters or longer. A few rowboats sought a way through the obstructions close to the houses. Then a small motorboat came and then another one.

We peered in the half dark at the houses; in an upstairs window, a curtain moved. The small boats jostled to find an embarkation place. The bigger ships lay somewhat farther away for anchor.

And so we fetched sixty people from the houses and the attics and brought them to the bigger ships, which were lying for anchor just outside the village.

Someone told us that one of the babies was born during the storm night, while the water was rising higher and higher. The mayor and the doctor came to help. The roof tiles were removed in the hope that if the water kept rising, the frame of the roof would separate and float. Now the young mother stood with her firstborn above the attic window. A small scaffold was built on the street (no boat could get there), but initially, she refused to hand over her child. "No way. You are not getting him." Strong men's hands brought her and the baby safely down, and then she coolly and cheerfully jumped into the *Spitfire*, beaming with joy about the great miracle that she survived that night of death and destruction.

It was low tide, and the water kept falling. Hastily the bigger ships with their valuable loads departed to Zierikzee or at least outside of the dike before they were grounded. A helicopter picked up some people by the church. At noon, the evacuation was completed. All of us together, among which were the strangest of boats, had been able to bring around 350 people to safety.

The *Spitfire* quickly made another round. "Hey, what are you doing there?" An eighty-four-year-old farmer, dressed in his Sunday best, was able to hide himself. "You are going with us, Opa. We will definitely take good care of you."

Off we went to Oosterland! "Just follow the tram rails," said Opa. The propeller of the boat struck the tram rails, cobblestones, poles, and gravel but enthusiastically kept on turning.

Our flooded road suddenly emerged to cross over a small inner dike and disappeared again into the water. It was a dry strip that was two hundred meters long and was as wide as the road. Here we found hundreds of people. We found a lieutenant of the Royal Dutch Navy, a Belgian Air Force officer in his sky-blue uniform, a tall and perfectly dressed captain of the British navy,[21] Green Beret shock troops, Red Cross soldiers, and the poor victims. There arrived the miracle: helicopter after helicopter landed on the strip; once in a while, three hung in the air behind each other to get a landing place.

In the meantime, an old grandma on a stretcher had been laid down under the spray hood of the *Spitfire*. Nowhere else was there protection against the lashing, cold wind. Once again we gave out of our supplies a warm meal, a couple of blankets, coffee, and cigarettes. Our grandpa's turn came up, and he went into a helicopter. When he was a couple of meters above the ground, he looked around with astonishment.

Then the Duwks arrived—amphibious vehicles that were the most perfect life savers during this moment of waters receding so fast even little rowboats were getting stuck. The American occupation army in Germany had sent them to Zeeland. They drove day and night; the officers were American, and the crews were German.[22]

Even for the Duwks, the number of refugees was too much. Somebody approached us and said, "I am from the Moorland Reclamation Society [*Heidemaatschappij*]. I know exactly where it is deep and not deep. Can't we go with your boat to Zierikzee?"

With seven men and two women, we embarked on the road back to Nieuwerkerk. We got stuck and got loose. We came across a horse whose front legs were hopelessly stuck in the mud of an invisible ditch; his owner, almost

---

[21]   His name was Captain Roger Casement, OBE, Royal Navy. He wrote us shortly thereafter: "The very sad experience in which the officers and men of the British Royal Navy were very proud to be able to render some little assistance . . . . It was only by chance that I was there at all. I had flown over the Isle of Schouwen-Duivenland from Zierikzee in a Belgian helicopter with the intention of seeing for myself the state of affairs and how best my craft of the Royal Naval Rhine Squadron could help. When I landed on the strip in question, I was immediately asked to give up my place to a number of old and ill people, including an expectant mother. This of course I willingly did, with the result that each time the helicopter returned, I was left behind. During this time I learned a great deal about the courage and fortitude of the Dutch people and their willingness to face up to the disaster that had overtaken them. The person who deserves a great deal of credit for the efficiency of the evacuation from that spot was Lieutenant Huizinga, Royal Dutch Navy, who worked untiringly directing the helicopters to land and arranging for their passengers. I have the greatest admiration for this officer (though I am afraid I may have spelt his name wrong)."

[22]   It was a little strange to suddenly see Germans again in their green-gray uniforms with heavy boots. A reporter wrote that some victims refused help and rather drowned. This is not true. The reporter was not there. The German boys helped where they could. They jumped into the ice-cold water to save people. Nothing was too much. And for this, they reaped silent tears of thanks.

to his neck in the water, tried to help him. It was low tide, and soon the salt water would rise three meters or so again with the high tide. We asked one the Duwks to help it out of its misery. We heard gunshots. A swimming dog willingly let itself be helped aboard. Then slowly but surely it became evident that the *Spitfire* would not be able to reach Zierikzee. In front of us, it was shallow. A night in an open boat was more than our passengers could handle, and thus we maneuvered our boat right in front of a Duwk so that they would have difficulty passing us.

"Bitte, nehmen Sie diese Leute mit, wir können nicht weiter."

"Unmöglich, wir sind ganz voll."

"Bitte, bitte [Please, please]."

"Schön den, aber ohne Gepäck."

Nevertheless, they took everything along—baggage and the little dog included.

With our crew of five, we stayed behind alone and motored back to the strip close to Oosterland to see what still needed to be done.

The evacuation of the refugees had ended. Only the Dutch naval officer, some Red Cross soldiers, and the shock troops remained. A second column of Duwks approached, under the command of an American major.[23] He could take all the Dutch people on board.

The Dutch naval officer came to the *Spitfire* and said, "Leave the boat here and come with the Duwks to Zierikzee."

I looked at the fishermen. They shook their heads.

"Do you know what the weather report is?" continued the naval officer.

"No," I answered. Our radio was, after all, left behind on the *Kil.*

"Storm out of the northwest. It really is better if you leave the boat here."

The fishermen kept silent.

"All right and good luck to you" are his farewell words.

We really could not join them. The *Ouddorp 5* lay unmanned—only its skipper was on board—for anchor outside the dike. It was in dangerous waters and directly exposed to the northwestern storm, which already announced itself with gusts of wind and snow showers.

When the darkness fell over the extended polder and the wind whipped up the gray water into white-capped waves, there were three little boats waging a desperate battle to reach the dike: an open steel botter from Volendam with seven men aboard, a fishing cutter from Groningen, and the *Spitfire*. We

---

[23]   Later we heard that this major fell into the ice-cold water. As a result of this fall, Queen Juliana complimented him on the work that his troops had done, but he had lost his voice and could not answer her.

navigated at the front of the group, searching for the best route. Suddenly, we got bundled up in telephone poles and wires. The cutter crashed full force into us. With a bang, its mast broke off. Once again, we went "full speed" ahead. There was a breach in the dike. The high tide rushed in, yet Willem de Vreugd and the young fishermen, with great adroitness and by using eddies and whirlpools, brought the boat outside. The botter went for anchor in front of the breach, but the current was too strong; the little boat was dragged along and disappeared from sight.

I looked at the fishermen and pointed to the east: "Bruinisse?"

They shook their heads and pointed to the west, where the North Sea is. "There the *Ouddorp 5* most likely will be for anchor." And that way we sailed; a howling wind, black clouds, snow showers, hail, foam, spray, and the full tide against us.

After hours of misery, a light appeared on the horizon. Yes, it was the *Ouddorp 5* with a botter next to it. There was a happy reunion in the small cabin. Then suddenly, the heavy ropes that tied the other botter to us broke. A moment later, it disappeared into the night.

Outside, it was so wild that I didn't believe I would ever see the *Spitfire* again. The skipper decided to bring up the spare anchor; the situation was that dangerous. With infinite care and patience, the heavy monster was retrieved, secured to the cables, secured the shackles by the men who for three days had not slept and were soaking wet. The fishermen did not want to speak while working, and when they did, they preferred to speak with biblical texts.[24] Now I heard them occasionally say something while I lay undressed in the small cabin (*undressed* means I had my cap and sea boots off).

"It is enormous bad weather."

"The ocean is vicious."

"Lower the second anchor."

"It is not going too well."

Indeed, I did not have much more to contribute. Here were men working, carried on by a tradition of centuries and hardened by the eternal fight against the elements.

Like all nights, an end came to this night. The *Spitfire* danced the next morning joyfully on two professionally laid cables. (There were two due to the fact that the tide turned itself against the storm during the night.)

---

[24]   In those days, we had someone on board who, perhaps due to nervousness, talked too much. I heard one of the fishermen say to his mate, "Lamentations 3:28." After coming home, we looked it up and found, "He can sit quietly in solitude and silence."

We had a short farewell. In the dark during a black downpour, the *Spitfire* sailed to Bruinisse—to the tramharbor of Zijpe.

There we found hundreds upon hundreds of assistance vessels. The hospital-church ship *De Hoop* sailed by; it was under the command of Skipper Willem Rog.

Where could we still help? Nowhere. The steam-roller of the national and international cooperation had eliminated the need for flat-bottomed boats. Further help lays on a different level.

We wrote the above after we had safely returned to Bentveld and got into our warm, highly situated, and dry bungalow (minus one chimney). And just like Great-Great-Grandfather Maurits Cornelis—who used a foreign language, Latin, in his journal occasionally for special events—we wrote at the end of the account: "Messieurs, à vous tous, le grand Salut d'Honneur!"

This is the end of our chronicle.

Sadly, an unadulterated portrait of the family could not be achieved. Our ancestors did their best to record all the good and positive they accomplished on paper. They did take care not to report anything bad about themselves. We highly regret this. We very much would have liked to include a chapter about our family's black sheep in our story! In a family as large as ours, dramas should have occurred. Black sheep and rakes were present. Today one can still hear a few old aunts whispering about an incident of earlier times, only to stop immediately when a cousin enters the room even though he has passed fifty years of age. They are thus legends that are difficult to recoup and are with little historical importance.

So it was in 1848 that a Van Hall who was a young student had racked up three thousand guilders in debt. When his father discovered this, he gave him the money. But instead of repaying his debt, he hired a coach with two horses and made a tour of Germany with some friends. They stayed in a small town where their night sleep was roughly disturbed by a number of rioters who were holding a demonstration. The uprising of 1848 was, after all, in full force. This annoyed our student, and while dressed in his nightshirt, he went to a balcony that overlooked the square. He roared at the crowd, "Schweinhunde, haltet die Maule!" upon which they slinked away. In Amsterdam, a very angry father awaited him—this time not with money but a one-way ticket to America.

Another case involved Floris Adriaan van Hall, Esq., who lived from 1829 to 1868. He was the consignee appointed to collect monies for Goor, Terborg, and Druten respectively. He was such a rake that twice he was recommended for dismissal. But twice the king refused because he did not want to offend the godfather, Minister Floris; a transfer was the solution. What the misdeeds entailed, the family hushed up.

The family continues to expand. Opa alone has over 150 descendants. Many live in the Netherlands, but you can find them almost throughout the whole world, especially in the United States and South America.

The mutual ties have remained strong. The first names of the ancestors are honored. In every branch, there are young people who are called Maurits, Floris, or Adriaan.

With these names, if I remember well, we started our story three centuries ago.

Bentveld, 1955–1959

ACKNOWLEDGMENTS

Some years ago, I thought I had written an engaging account of the family, but when I gave Godfried Bomans a chapter to read, nothing was left untouched. In very sharp words, he pointed out many shortcomings. He gave me a long list of new resources. I am extremely grateful for his wise lessons and for the trouble he took upon himself. Without Godfried Bomans, *Three Centuries* would never have seen a printed version.

I owe thanks to Elsa, my wife. Her patience was stretched to the limit. I worked in our bedroom, and books, papers, and writings slowly took over all the space there. They also took over her bed, so she had to find her night rest elsewhere in the house. Nobody was allowed to touch anything. The windows stayed shut for fear of playful gusts of wind. Worse was the fact that I, not only with her but also with everyone else I met, spoke about the book too often; I was hopeful that such talks would lead to new leads and sources. I had become, what one calls in English, a bore. On one occasion, this became apparent to me when I was invited to an official dinner in honor of some foreign visitors. Per the old custom, my eyes wandered over the guests; I thought that perhaps there was someone present who could offer up something new. Evidently, the hostess noticed this because she pulled me aside and said, "Maurits, please do not talk this evening about that book of the family." "It will not cross my mind," I answered not quite truthfully. It is fitting that I offer here an apology to the many that I bothered, and it is also fitting that I give a word of gratitude to the countless people who, in fact, helped.

I will, in particular, mention J. B. van Hall, Esq., the librarian of the Royal Institute of the Tropics (*Koninklijk Instituut voor de Tropen*); Ms. Dr. I. H. van Eeghen, the deputy archivist of Amsterdam; Dr. S. Hart, the principal archivist of Amsterdam; C. C. van Valkenburg, Esq.; G. B. Pelikaan, the mayor of Vianen; Yvonne Verspijck; Dame C. de Jonge van Ellemeet, the librarian of the Groote Club; the lunch table of Leo Koene in the Groote Club; the Managing Board of the Shipping Association North (*Scheepvaart Vereniging Noord*); J. Korstenhorst; and my son John.

And finally, I would like to give a word of thanks to my forefathers who so carefully and with great diligence described their experiences.

This family tree serves only as a tool to help the reader with the story of the ancestors. For the official family tree, which covers many pages, we must refer the reader to the Nederlands Patriciaat 24th edition. The names of the family members who are mentioned in the book are printed in bold.

Key Dutch words translated:
Gehuwd = married
Ongehuwd = single
Tweelingszuster = twin sister
Kaapvaarder en Zeerover = privateer and pirate
Geen Kinderen = no children

Jan Willem
1727 - 1804
4 maal gehuwd
eenzaam in Bengalen overleden

Sophia Maria
1730 - 1789
ongehuwd

Adriaan Teyler van Hall
Kerkmeester, Kaapvaarder
en Zeerover, 1761 - 1839
1e huwelijk 1783 E. R. Teyler
2e huwelijk 1786 C. M. van Markel
2 kinderen uit 2e huwelijk

Hermannus
Patriot en Predikant
bij familia Van der Capellen
1763 - 1841
gehuwd 1798 C. Assink
5 kinderen

Abraham Floris
1764 - 1803
⊠ Yvica (Balearen)⊠
gehuwd 1792 A. C. Post
geen kinderen

Jan Everard
1765 - 1766⌐

Floris Adriaan
de Minister 1791 - 1866
1e huwelijk 1815 A. P. Bondt
2e huwelijk 1853
H. M. J. Baronesse Schimmelpenninck van der Oye
geen kinderen

Johanna Maria
1792 - 1796

Adriaan
1793 - 1851
gehuwd 1819 Margaretha
Klinkhamer 12 kinderen
l
Maurits Cornelis
vriend Multatuli
1822 - 1889

1e huwelijk

Anna Jacoba 1805 - 1895 gehuwd A. Ch. Van Braam Houckgeest
Johanna Petronella 1806 - 1848 gehuwd Prof. Dr J. Tideman
Wijnanda Jacoba 1811 - 1876 ongehuwd
M. H Cornelia 1814 - 1884 gehuwd P. M. Jongeneel
A. P. Florentine 1817 - 1901 gehuwd Mr Otto Braat Bisdom, Heer van Cattenbroek

2e huwelijk

Anne M. Cornelis
1865 -1911
gehuwd 1890 C. S. de Bode
5 kinderen

Jan
1866 - 1940
gehuwd 1895 Hester Boissevain
dochter Ch. Boissevain
Alg. Handelsblad
(Vader Jan en Moeder Hessie)

Hel. Suzanna
1869 - 1928
gehuwd 1893 Gijsbert van
Tienhoven
3 kinderen
Sonja
gehuwd Bob Boissevain
⊠ 1945 Bergen Belsen

Floris Adriaan
1870 - 1941
gehuwd 1904 Jonkvrouwe
C. M. van Panhuys
2 kinderen

Maurits C.
1895 - 1944
⊠ Birma-spoorweg

Frederik (Frits)
Beeldhouwer
1899 - 1944
⊠ in Duitsland

P. G. Johanna (Nelleke)
1897 - 1939
1e huwelijk 1921 René de Monchy
2e huwelijk 1931 Jacques Dutilh

Debora (Dea)
1899 -

Maria
1900 -
1e huwelijk 1924 Frans van Oyen ⊠
2e huwelijk Wiete Hopperus Buma

Floris Adriaan
1902 -
gehuwd 1932 Olga Heldring

FREDERIK MAURITS
1896 - 1915
adelborst
(Freddy)

John
1899 -

Maurits Cornelis
1901-
(de auteur)
gehuwd Elsa Tingulstad, 1906 -
geadopteerd 1916
door H. P. Davis, USA.

John
Sonja
Michael
Ellen

Hilda Gerarda 1902
Eugen 1906
André 1907
Charles E. H. 1911
Eylard Fr. M. 1915

Marlene
geboren 1930

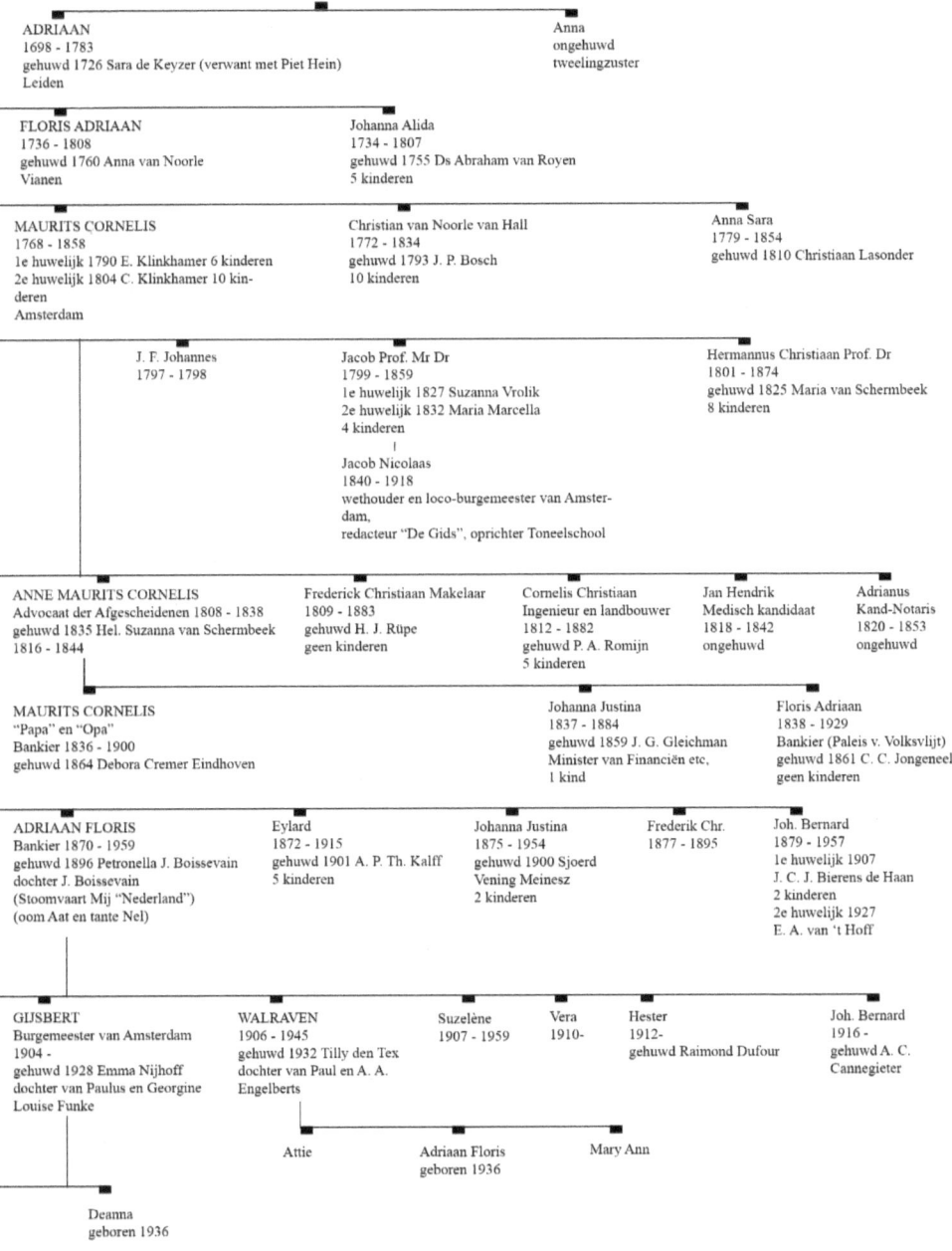

FLORIS ALLERTZOON van Hall
1661 - 1709
gehuwd 1692 Aaltje de Wilde
Arnhem - Leiden

ADRIAAN
1698 - 1783
gehuwd 1726 Sara de Keyzer (verwant met Piet Hein)
Leiden

Anna
ongehuwd
tweelingzuster

FLORIS ADRIAAN
1736 - 1808
gehuwd 1760 Anna van Noorle
Vianen

Johanna Alida
1734 - 1807
gehuwd 1755 Ds Abraham van Royen
5 kinderen

MAURITS CORNELIS
1768 - 1858
1e huwelijk 1790 E. Klinkhamer 6 kinderen
2e huwelijk 1804 C. Klinkhamer 10 kinderen
Amsterdam

Christian van Noorle van Hall
1772 - 1834
gehuwd 1793 J. P. Bosch
10 kinderen

Anna Sara
1779 - 1854
gehuwd 1810 Christiaan Lasonder

J. F. Johannes
1797 - 1798

Jacob Prof. Mr Dr
1799 - 1859
1e huwelijk 1827 Suzanna Vrolik
2e huwelijk 1832 Maria Marcella
4 kinderen
|
Jacob Nicolaas
1840 - 1918
wethouder en loco-burgemeester van Amsterdam,
redacteur "De Gids", oprichter Toneelschool

Hermannus Christiaan Prof. Dr
1801 - 1874
gehuwd 1825 Maria van Schermbeek
8 kinderen

ANNE MAURITS CORNELIS
Advocaat der Afgescheidenen 1808 - 1838
gehuwd 1835 Hel. Suzanna van Schermbeek
1816 - 1844

Frederick Christiaan Makelaar
1809 - 1883
gehuwd H. J. Rüpe
geen kinderen

Cornelis Christiaan
Ingenieur en landbouwer
1812 - 1882
gehuwd P. A. Romijn
5 kinderen

Jan Hendrik
Medisch kandidaat
1818 - 1842
ongehuwd

Adrianus
Kand-Notaris
1820 - 1853
ongehuwd

MAURITS CORNELIS
"Papa" en "Opa"
Bankier 1836 - 1900
gehuwd 1864 Debora Cremer Eindhoven

Johanna Justina
1837 - 1884
gehuwd 1859 J. G. Gleichman
Minister van Financiën etc,
1 kind

Floris Adriaan
1838 - 1929
Bankier (Paleis v. Volksvlijt)
gehuwd 1861 C. C. Jongeneel
geen kinderen

ADRIAAN FLORIS
Bankier 1870 - 1959
gehuwd 1896 Petronella J. Boissevain
dochter J. Boissevain
(Stoomvaart Mij "Nederland")
(oom Aat en tante Nel)

Eylard
1872 - 1915
gehuwd 1901 A. P. Th. Kalff
5 kinderen

Johanna Justina
1875 - 1954
gehuwd 1900 Sjoerd
Vening Meinesz
2 kinderen

Frederik Chr.
1877 - 1895

Joh. Bernard
1879 - 1957
1e huwelijk 1907
J. C. J. Bierens de Haan
2 kinderen
2e huwelijk 1927
E. A. van 't Hoff

GIJSBERT
Burgemeester van Amsterdam
1904 -
gehuwd 1928 Emma Nijhoff
dochter van Paulus en Georgine
Louise Funke

WALRAVEN
1906 - 1945
gehuwd 1932 Tilly den Tex
dochter van Paul en A. A.
Engelberts

Suzelène
1907 - 1959

Vera
1910-

Hester
1912-
gehuwd Raimond Dufour

Joh. Bernard
1916 -
gehuwd A. C.
Cannegieter

Attie

Adriaan Floris
geboren 1936

Mary Ann

Deanna
geboren 1936

Index of Proper Names

BIBLIOGRAPHY

- some of the written material consulted

Het geslacht Van Hall	A. A. Vosterman van Oyen.
Nederland's Patriciaat	Jaargang 1911.
Idem.	Jaargang 1938 bewerkt door W. van Maanen.
Reis naar het Oosten (1720 – 1723)	Uitgegeven door J. W. Heyman, gedrukt in 1757 door A. Kalleweer, Leiden.
Het Land van Vianen	P. Horden Jz.
Recht en Slecht in het land van Brederode	Idem.
Manuaal van de Geërfden van Heicop en Boeicop	Adriaan van Hall, 1768–1858
Dagboek	van M. C. van Hall, 1768–1858.
Hendrik, Graaf van Brederode, Medegrondlegger der Nederlandsche Vrijheid verdedigd door	Mr M. C. van Hall, Staatsraad, etc.
Antwoord aan Mr M. C. van Hall over Brederode	Mr G. Groen van Prinsterer.

Herinneringen van Mr M. C. van Hall   Mr M. C. van Hall.
1787–1815

Rutger Jan Schimmelpenninck
vrnl. Als Bataafsch Afgezant bij het   Idem.
Vredescongres te Amiens in 1802

Het Leven en Karakter van Admiraal
Jhr Jan Hendrik van Kinsbergen   Idem.

De Familie Falck in den Patriottentijd
en de reis van Anton Reinhard Falck
uit het bezitte gebied van Holland naar
Frankrijk in het jaar 1795   Dr J. C. H. de Pater.

Mr M. C. van Hall als letterkundige   Dr E. Cohen
   Gedr. Govers – Maassluis 1928.

Levensbericht Mr M. C. van Hall   Mr H. J. Koenen, Jan. 1859.

Geschiedenis van Nederland na 1830   Jhr Mr. J. de Bosch Kemper.

Mr F. A. van Hall als Minister   Mr J. G. Gleichman.

Gedichten, 1818   Mr M. C. van Hall.

Dichterlijk Geschenk, 1854   Idem.

Familie Herinneringen   Prof. Dr H. C. van Hall.

Levensbericht van Mr Jacob van Hall   Prof. Dr J. de Wal.

Een korte, maar moeilijke levensdag.
Anne Maurits Cornelis van Hall,
de advocaat der vervolgende
afgescheidenen   J. Bosch, Geref. Pred. te Steenwijk.

Brandende Harten De Geschiedenis van Maurits en Suze van Hall	Gera Kraan – van den Burg.
Willem de Clercq naar zijn dagboek	A. Pierson.
Het Réveil in Nederland	M. E. Kluit.
Onze Voortrekkers, de Geschiedenis van eenige leden der familie Boissevain	Charles Boissevain.
Van Dag tot Dag, verzamelde opstellen	Charles Boissevain.
Stamboek der Boissevains	Barthold Hubert Boissevain.
Herinneringen	Mr H. P. G. Quack
Prof Mr Dr. Jacob van Hall	B. J. L. de Geer.
Levensbericht van Floris Adriaan van Hall, Heer van Heicop en Boeicop 1838–1929	Lofrede op zichzelf, na vrijsprekend vonnis, gedrukt in 1904.
De beeldhouwer F. J. van Hall 1899–1945	Met een voorwoord van Mari Andriessen.
Het Dagboek van de Student Nicolaas Beets	Dr H. E. van Gelder.
Paviljoen van Glas	M. Revis.
Engel van de Stadt, 1746–1819, Zijn voor en zijn nageslacht	Uitgegeven door A. A. M. Stols 1951.

Walraven van Hall, 10 Februari 1906–12 Februari 1945	gedrukt na de oorlog 1940–1945.
Geschiedenis van Nederland	N. V. Uitgeverij Joost van den Vondel.
Mijn Leven	Walrave Boissevain.
Dossier Van Hall	Gemeente-archief, Amsterdam.